CATHY BECK'S
FLY-FISHING
HANDBOOK

CATHY BECK'S
FLY-FISHING
HANDBOOK

• • •

CATHY BECK

•

ILLUSTRATED
BY
ROD WALINCHUS

LYONS & BURFORD, PUBLISHERS

Printed in the United States of America

10 9 8 7 6 5 4 3 2 1

Interior Design by: Howard P. Johnson, Communigrafix, Inc.

Typesetting and Composition by: Sam Sheng, CompuDesign

Library of Congress Cataloging-in-Publication Data

Beck, Cathy.
     Fly fishing handbook
     Cathy Beck's fly fishing handbook / Cathy Beck; illustrated by Rod Walinchus.
          p.   cm
     Includes bibliographical references and index.

     ISBN 1-55821-471-2 (paperback); 1-55821-340-6 (cloth)
     1. Fly fishing—Handbooks, manuals, etc.   I. Title.
     799. 1'2—dc20   95-44809
                                                                    CIP

TO MY HUSBAND, BARRY,

who took a year off from fishing so he could stand by my side as my private guide and instructor and teach me. I learned more during that first year than possibly all the years since. He taught me patience and perserverance. I owe my fly fishing to him—my best friend and my business partner.

TO MY DAUGHTER, ANNIE,

who generously gave up her mother and accepted her grandmother as a stand-in for countless school plays, class trips, band concerts, May Days, and school functions, so that I could travel and fish with our work. She has been lucky and happy to grow up in her grandparents' home as much as her own. I couldn't have lived with the guilt had she been unhappy about any of it.

TO MY PARENTS.

My fishing started at home with them. I cannot imagine myself fishing as an adult without the endless summers as a child exploring and fishing the ponds on our farm. It certainly wasn't sophisticated fishing—my sister and I used anything we could think of: bread, worms, bugs, and later spinning rods with spinning lures. But those years taught me about the habits of fish, worms, frogs, snakes, mud, and being dirty. I was a very happy kid and my parents made that possible.

CONTENTS

ACKNOWLEDGMENTS
viii

FOREWORD BY LEFTY KREH
ix

ACKNOWLEDGMENTS

Nick Lyons came to me two years ago with a book idea. Without his encouragement and gentle nudging, I wouldn't have completed the project. He told me that writing a book is like fishing a big river: you get in and take it one step at a time. Nick, Dianne Russell, Anja Schmidt, and everyone at Lyons & Burford made this book happen.

Rod Walinchus agreed to do thirty illustrations, and throughout the months the number mushroomed. He never once reminded me of the original agreement, although I'm sure he remembered. I thank Rod for his help, patience, and suggestions throughout the project. The chapter openings were his idea and I think they are a wonderful addition.

Lefty Kreh said, "Woman, you gotta do it," when I talked to him about the book idea. Whenever I needed anything, Lefty was there. He always has time for me. He's the busiest person I know, and yet the best friend anyone could have.

And all our friends, far and wide, who from the beginning accepted me as one of the fishermen.

FOREWORD

One factor I find so welcome in the world of fly fishing is the number of women who are now enjoying the sport. A few years ago it was rare to see a woman fly fishing unless she was accompanying her boyfriend or spouse. Today, this is no longer true. In lodges I have visited in the past several years all around the world, and in the seminars I conduct in this country and abroad, it is not unusual for at least one-third of the participants to be women. All of them are very much interested in learning more about this sport.

There are good reasons why women are finding fly fishing so enjoyable. Most women today between the ages of twenty and fifty work outside the home. When they get a vacation, they would like to spend it with their husband or boyfriend doing something both enjoy. Fly fishing fits that bill perfectly. Few fly fishermen are competitive. Instead of competing against other anglers, they enjoy sharing experiences. The average fly fisherman who meets another on the stream has found a friend. He will share information and even flies so both of them can have a good time. Most women do not want to join a sport where participants are competing against one another.

Fortunately, fly casting, even with big rods for billfish and tarpon, does not require muscular force if one learns to cast properly. There are plenty of women fly fishers who have proven this. Fly fishing is done in pretty places, and that is certainly a plus. These are just some of the reasons why women are flocking to the sport.

Cathy Beck has written this book about fly fishing, but it is not just a book for women. She is such an accomplished fly fisher that both women and men can learn much from its pages. The contents cover all phases of the sport, from selecting your gear to special saltwater fishing situations.

Not only is Cathy a highly qualified freshwater angler (she spends time each year in Alaska and in the West) but she has caught bigger snook than have most men (twenty-three pounds), tarpon, bonefish, even permit on the fly. She writes from firsthand experience, and although I know women will enjoy and profit from reading this book, I feel sure their spouses will benefit from Cathy's knowledge as well.

LEFTY KREH

1

THE PLEASURES
OF **FLY FISHING**

I BELIEVE THAT ONE OF THE GREATEST ATTRAC-
tions to fly fishing is that we don't have to be great athletes
to be good fly fishermen. We can be on the receiving end
of tremendous fun and fulfillment without having to
undergo any physical training or work up a sweat in a
gymnasium trying to kick the pants off an opponent. We
get exercise, fresh air, and can go to some absolutely beautiful places to enjoy the sport. To most of us, water is very
relaxing, whether we're on a dock, in a boat, or standing
in a stream in our waders, just being there with nature
along a favorite trout stream, in a bluegill pond, or on a
flat in the salt water.

Some of the best advice I've ever heard about getting started in fly fishing came from Dave Whitlock, noted author, artist, and angler. I listened as Dave told a group of new fly fishermen to spend half their money on good instruction and the rest on equipment. I couldn't agree more. Good instruction will save you a lot of time and frustration. I don't think it's necessary to spend a lot of money on tackle, but I do believe that you need good basic equipment. It's impossible to enjoy fishing if you're clumping around in a pair of heavy men's waders that are miles too big or trying to stuff everything that should be in a fishing vest in the pockets of your jacket. We have reasonably priced graphite outfits (rod, reel, and line combinations) that are much easier to use than the fiberglass rods of a few years ago. Make a commitment, buy the best you can afford, and you'll be off to a good start.

Take to heart the advice you'll read in chapter 5. Being comfortable with your casting and knowing how to use your gear is crucial to becoming a good fisherman. By putting in time and effort in the beginning, you'll be rewarded with a sport that you can enjoy for the rest of your life. As a woman fisherman, I believe that women have to be good (not expert) to be accepted and respected in what is still a man's sport.

There seems to be a lot of discussion today on what we women who fish should call ourselves. I myself am happy being a fly fisherman. I know women who prefer to be called fly fishers or fly anglers. "Fly fisherman" comes naturally to me, and I don't feel the need to be gender-specific in how I refer to myself. Therefore, "fly fisherman" is my term of choice throughout this book. I'm the first one to insist on waders that are designed to fit women or wading shoes built on a woman's last, but I'm content to be a fly fisherman. The choice is yours.

It's easy today to learn to fly fish. Women are being welcomed and encouraged to join Trout Unlimited and Federation of Fly Fishers chapters and other fishing clubs. These are excellent organizations and often offer instruction in both fly casting and fly tying. The meetings provide a great opportunity to learn of places to fish, and you may even meet some new fishing friends.

Get to know your local fly shops. The clerks always know where the best fishing is and what flies to use. They can also help you select gear and equipment. If you don't feel comfortable with the first shop you try, find another one. Be confident, and let them know you're seriously interested in fly fishing. Many times we are overlooked because some clerks assume we don't fish and must be in the shop with someone who does. But most clerks are happy to help men and women—the success of their shop depends on it.

Ask about regional books and videos that may be available. Charles Meck, for instance, has written a book on fly fishing in Pennsylvania, and in it he lists all the trout streams, what flies to use, when to go, and even where to park the car! And there are books like his for almost any part of the country. If you're still unsure, consider hiring a guide for the first couple of outings. Make sure the guide knows ahead of time that you're new to fly fishing and will need help. A local fly shop can make these arrangements. Having a guide is like having a private tutor for the day who can provide a wealth of information. He'll show you where to fish, what flies to use, how to handle the fish, how to approach the fish, and the best times to fish. He can also suggest places where you can fish on your own. (Yes, there *are* women guides, though not a great many at this point.) In short, you can find out in a couple of days with a guide what could take months or years on your own.

Buy fly-fishing magazines and send for advertised mail-order catalogs. Study these catalogs and become familiar with available tackle and products. Women have equipment designed just for us today, from waders and wading shoes to fishing vests. And it's not just the same old thing painted pink. Manufacturers are paying attention to women who fish and are giving us well-designed, functional products that fit properly and are fun to use.

If you want to be taken seriously, you have to approach the sport seriously. Watch the good fishermen (the ones catching the fish). They will often be dressed in conservative colors, especially on trout streams. This doesn't mean drab colors but rather greens, tans, blues, dark purples, deep violets, and dark reds. These colors blend in with the surroundings in most freshwater environments. Bright colors will set you apart from the serious fishermen, not to mention that you may scare the fish. White and pink shirts and caps may be fine on a saltwater flat but could spell disaster on a small trout stream.

Look around for ponds and lakes that are close to home. The hunting and fishing editor of your local newspaper is a good person to contact. The information that accompanies most fishing licenses will often include suggestions on regional fishing.

It's easy to get caught up in the world of the workplace, the telephone, the home, and the family. Take an hour and fish for bluegills and other panfish. You won't believe how much fun it is—the fish are usually cooperative, it's great hooking and casting practice, and you'll feel good about your success. If you have home water, you are lucky indeed. This might be a local bluegill pond, a lagoon or lake, or a nearby trout or bass stream. It's any water that you can get to easily and can fish often.

A fisherman, over time, becomes very comfortable with her home water. You learn where the best fishing spots are, you know the ledges, the holes, where the big rocks are, and you get to know the fish and how they behave. You know the best times to fish and you feel safe. In a way, it feels like it's yours, and in a way, it is.

It's like having a good friend: you can let your guard down because you know it so well. There are no surprises. Like a good friend, you go through the ups and downs. High water, low water, pollution, fish kills, people who leave their garbage, maybe the threat of water diversion for human use, or even development. You just never know, but you rejoice in it during good times and cry for it during bad times.

As a new fisherman, you may not know where your home water is yet. But once you find it, you'll have hours and hours of fun, rewarding experiences ahead. And it's not all one-sided. Your home water has gained a friend, too. When you pick up someone else's garbage or fight against pollution or development, you're showing you care, and maybe you can help make a difference.

New water is another story. The unknown can be exciting, like a new love. If it's a positive experience, you look forward to the next time, and you'll want to return. It doesn't have to mean catching fish. It might be a beautiful mountain stream with moss-covered ledges dripping with fresh rain, ferns, and crystal-clear tumbling pocket water—but maybe no fish the day you're there. The beauty alone will make you want to go back.

On the other hand, if you get to a new stream and the water is high and muddy and it's a rainy, cold, gray day, you may get back in the car thinking that you don't see anything so special about this stream! A couple of days later, after the water has cleared and dropped and the sun is out with the birds singing, it will be a different stream! So don't always go on first impressions. We have days when we're not at our best, and so does fishing.

If you don't feel safe, well, that's another story. I would never go back alone to a place that I felt was unsafe, regardless of the fishing. Whether it's water conditions or people who present the threat, care should be taken to avoid such situations.

Fly fishing is therapeutic for the mind and body, and one of the nicest things about it is that you can enjoy it by yourself or with a friend. Sometimes you just need some space, and this sport can give it to you. On the other hand, it's a wonderful sport to enjoy with a special someone or with other friends. Women find fly casting very rewarding. Perhaps it's the delicate balance of timing, rhythm, and motion or perhaps the artistically dressed flies instead of bait, or maybe because the fish can be released and returned unharmed to the water. Or maybe it's for all these reasons.

How serious a fly fisherman you become is up to you. You may apply yourself to fishing seriously whenever you go, or you may want a good book for the slow times. You may fish during the nice weather and avoid the rain or cold. The important part is that you enjoy the time you spend fishing. Just about any kind of weather can be endured and even enjoyed with modern fabrics and functional clothes.

I recall one day on the Bighorn River in Montana when the ice was freezing in the rod guides, the snow had been falling steadily since sometime the night before, misty fog was hanging gently over the water, and the fish were everywhere sipping in tiny mayflies called Tricos. It's one of my favorite memories. I was dressed for the weather, and the fishing was any fly fisherman's dream—lots of insects and lots of rising fish!

Fly fishing can take us to many wonderful places. A man once told me that he travels so he can fish in different places. In the next breath, his wife said she fishes so she can travel with him to those places. Think about it. They have a wonderful time together, they travel and fish and are enjoying both—from two different angles. And there's nothing wrong with either view. Fly fishing has taken me to Alaska, Labrador, Nova Scotia, the Bahamas, Mexico, British Columbia, all over the United States, and I always want to go back to all of these places. And I do return to many of them over and over again.

Fly fishing is a lot of things to a lot of people. Whether you walk down to the dock after dinner and cast in the pond or travel to some exotic destination in a remote corner of the globe, fly fishing is there waiting for you. It's a chance to explore a whole new world full of fun and adventure. I hope this book helps get you there.

2

FLY-FISHING TACKLE: RODS AND REELS

WHEN FLY FISHERMEN TALK ABOUT THEIR
"outfits," they are referring to the combination of the fly
rod, fly reel, fly line, and leader. We'll talk about fly lines
and leaders in chapter 4, so let's look first at rods and reels.

RODS

To be recognized and accepted as a creditable fly fisherman,
we must understand two important tools: rods and reels.

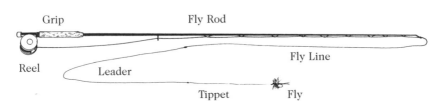

A complete rod outfit with line and leader.

Simply put, the fly rod is a flexible lever. It uses the energy our arm gives to the cast to deliver the fly to the fish.

Beginning at the bottom of the rod, the *butt cap* holds the reel. Some- times, on lighter rods, the *butt cap* is replaced with two slid- ing bands. The *reel seat* is easy to remember because it is where the reel sits on the rod. It may be made of cork, wood, or metal. Usually rods intended for lighter fish (trout, as opposed to, say, tarpon) will have reel seats of cork or wood. Heavier rods will have anodized aluminum reel seats.

If the rod has a *butt cap* (and not all do), then this butt cap becomes part of the reel seat because the *reel foot* will slide into the butt cap. Otherwise, the reel may be held in place by two sim- ple sliding bands, each one holding an end of the reel foot (see the reel photograph on page 8), or by a down-locking or up-locking reel seat. Up-locking, as implied, simply means that the reel is held with hardware that screws up, toward the rod. Down-locking is just the opposite: it screws down, toward the butt cap, and holds the reel in place. This hardware, whatever the style, may have different finishes. Hardware intended for fresh water is often shiny, polished-looking nickel silver or flat black anodized alu- minum. Anodized aluminum is almost always used in salt water because it is less susceptible corrosion.

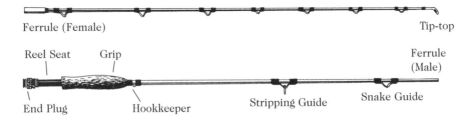

The parts of a fly rod.

Real Seats A: up-locking,   B: down-locking,   C: slide-band

Continuing up the rod, the *handle* is made up of a series of cork rings that are glued together and sanded for a comfortable grip. The length of the handle is determined by how many cork rings are used. If you look closely, you can count the rings. Occasionally on less-expensive rods you may see a preformed molded handle, but most handles are of cork.

The *hookkeeper* is located just above the handle and is standard equipment on most rods. This little ring can at times resemble a *line guide*. But the line does not go through the hookkeeper—ever! When the rod is together, string line through the guides, then tie the fly on. Hook the fly into the hookkeeper, reel in the slack line, and your outfit will be ready to transport. The hookkeeper simply keeps the line from tangling around the rod.

The first guide that the line goes through is the *stripping guide*. Depending on the size of the rod, there may be two stripping guides. This will be a heavy-duty guide and will look "beefed-up" compared to the other guides. Often the stripping guide will have a ceramic lining. This guide takes the wear and tear and friction of the fly line traveling back and forth to and from the fly reel, thus the additional armoring.

The other guides, decreasing in size as the rod diameter decreases, are called *snake guides*. The guide at the top is simply called the *tip-top*. Check your guides at least once a year. After a lot of use, they can develop sharp little grooves that can actually cut into and ruin fly lines. The fly line traveling back and forth over and over causes the grooves that can ruin the line. Worn guides can be replaced by a rod repair person through your local fly shop.

The connection where rod sections join together is the *fer-rule*. Two-piece rods will have one ferrule, and multiple-piece rods may have two or three ferrules, or even more. Looking close-ly at the ferrule, one can easily see that there is a male ferrule and a female ferrule. The narrower male ferrule should be snugly fit-ted into the larger female. This has to be a snug fit or the tip of the rod will come off during casting. (On the other hand, don't jam them together so tightly that you can't get them apart.)

It's very important that the ferrules be kept clean. Today's ferrule materials don't require any special treatment or mainte-nance. But grains of sand or even a strand of hair can cause prob-lems in ferrules because of the close tolerances. The easiest way to keep the ferrules clean is to put the rod in its cloth sleeve and tube as soon as you take it apart. This is always the safest place for the rod whenever you're not fishing with it.

Fly rods are available in a lot of different lengths and line sizes for different fishing situations. For most freshwater fish (trout, panfish, light bass) a rod from seven feet nine inches to nine feet will be fine. Rods in this range are also the easiest to use when you are learning to cast. Rods shorter than this are, for the most part, designed for small brushy streams in close quarters or for special tests of skill by advanced anglers. On the other hand, a longer rod may be quite comfortable on a big lake, in the surf, or casting from a boat where we have plenty of room. My first rod was eight and a half feet, and that's still my overall favorite rod length.

Eventually, we find that one rod will not do everything for us. If we fish mostly ponds and medium-sized streams, we may find that our eight-and-a-half-foot rod is just right. Then we might have the opportunity to fish on a small, mountain brook, trout stream and it may suddenly be too long, always getting tangled in the brush and branches. Or, we may be invited along to fish a big river like the Delaware in New York or the Bighorn in Montana, where a nine-foot rod will be to our advantage, giving us more leverage and control with longer casts.

We should always start with a rod suitable for the kind of fish-ing we'll be doing the most, and branch out from there. It's like buying shoes: one pair won't do for everything. We need different shoes for different occasions. Sneakers may be fine for working in the garden, but they won't do for the opera; our heels may not be quite right for the local fishing-club meeting, and open-toed shoes aren't good for winter. Fly rods are available in various lengths, but overall, rods in that seven-and-a-half-to-nine-foot range will be the ones you use most.

The rod length and line weight (described in chapter 4), along with other pertinent information, is often written just forward of the rod handle or on the butt cap. This information usually includes the manufacturer, a model name or number, what weight line to use, the rod length, and the weight of the rod blank.

ROD ACTION

Understanding rod action is an important part of understanding fly rods. Rod action merely means how much or how little the rod bends while casting. Simply put, the less the rod bends, the faster the line is able to travel back and forth during the cast.

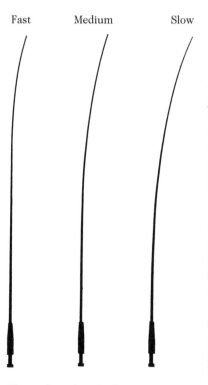

Fast   Medium   Slow

Although casting is described in much detail in chapter 5, we still need to think of the cast in order to understand rod action. Rod actions are generally referred to as slow, medium, or fast. *Slow-action* rods bend more, *fast-action* rods bend less, and *medium-action* rods fall in the middle. Where the rod does most of the bending will affect how the rod feels. A *tip-action* rod bends more in the tip. A *full-flex* rod bends from one end to the other with the tip bending more than the butt section. This type of action is also often referred to as *progressive action*. Rod manufacturers are able to incorporate desired actions into rod design.

If we were to limit our fishing to dry-fly fishing at long distances, most of us would want a faster-action rod. This rod would bend less, allowing us to accelerate line speed to achieve the longer distance of the cast. With the fast line speed, the fly would

Three flexed rods demonstrating different rod actions: slow, medium, and fast.

stay dry and float well for us. But because the line would travel very fast, it would be a difficult rod to fish closely with because the line would hit the water very hard and not allow a delicate presentation.

On the other hand, if we wanted to fish only wet flies, we would want a slow rod. This slow rod would bend more, giving us a slower cast to help keep the fly wet so it will sink easily. The slower cast would also have a wider *casting loop*, which would help us avoid tangling the leader; this is always a concern when fishing with split shot or heavily weighted flies.

The best of both worlds would be a medium-action rod. Medium-action rods are very popular because of their versatility.

It is important to cast a line on a rod before deciding whether to buy the rod or not. If the rod doesn't feel good when you're casting it, you won't enjoy using it. And what feels good to one fisherman may not feel good to another. Only by casting a rod can you be certain of how it will feel and perform.

Graphite is the preferred choice of rod materials today. Although we have talented rod makers building bamboo rods, and though fiberglass and boron rods have enjoyed periods of popularity, nothing compares to graphite. Graphite is lightweight and has varying degrees of stiffness and tensile strength, allowing manufacturers to offer rods in a vast array of lengths and actions.

FLY REELS

The fly reel has three major functions: it stores our line, provides drag when we need it, and helps balance the rod as we cast.

If the rod and reel are suitable for each other, the weight of the reel will help the rod feel balanced in your hand. The general rule of thumb is that the weight of the outfit should be roughly equalized when the rod is balanced just above the cork handle on your index finger. There is much less credence placed on this rule nowadays, and, generally, if the reel feels comfortable on the rod and casts well, that's more than good enough. (Obviously, a small trout reel would not balance on a tarpon rod. There is a lot to be said for common sense.)

If we had to, we could coil the line, hold it in one hand, and cast with the other hand. This immediately brings a few obvious problems to mind. We wouldn't be able to use our "line" hand for anything else (such as holding the fish, unhooking, releasing, or changing flies) because the coils of line would still have to be dealt with. We would have no *drag*, the mechanical means of putting pressure on the outgoing line, and the extra line would always be getting tangled when we were playing a fish. Because we would have to apply tension as needed with our hand on the line as we played the fish, it would be easy to cut our hands and fingers with fast-moving line, as well as break off the fish because of uneven tension on the leader.

So, for all the obvious reasons and more (it's something else to shop for!), the reel is an important part of our gear. Most reels today are made of different grades and variations of aluminum and occasionally graphite.

LEFT-HAND WIND OR RIGHT-HAND WIND?

To decide which hand you want to wind (or crank) the reel, you need to visualize casting. If you cast with your right hand, it's easy to reach down with your left to wind. The opposite is true if you're left-handed. Otherwise, if you want to wind the reel with the same hand you cast with, you can simply cast, hook the fish, then switch the rod to the other hand. This method is traditionally correct, but many of us find that switching hands with a fish on is more difficult than simply reeling with the other hand. Either way is acceptable.

Switching the direction that you wind is not as easy as turning the reel around on the rod. The line should always come off the bottom of the reel, and the crank should always be in the forward direction. If we simply turn the reel around and put it on the rod with the handle on the other side, the line would come out the back of the reel toward us instead of heading out to the stripping guide, and the crank would be backward. We would need to take the line and backing completely off the reel, wind it back on in the opposite direction, and change the drag and *line guard*.

If a line guard is used, it will be located where the line comes off the reel. Not all reels have line guards; sometimes the line comes out between two of the reel posts. The line guard cradles the line, forcing it off the center of the reel, and is usually of a strong metal to prevent the line from wearing a groove in the guard.

SPOOL DIAMETER AND SPOOL DEPTH

Spool diameter refers to the distance across the plate or surface

Deep (left) and shallow (right) reel spools.

of the reel (think of a twelve-inch pizza). The *spool depth* refers to how far apart the two reel plates are placed. A reel may have a *narrow* or a *deep* spool. Obviously, the deep spool can hold more line than can the shallow spool.

For most freshwater fishing, a spool diameter of about three inches is ideal. The larger the diameter of the coiled line on the reel spool, the faster we can retrieve it when we wind the reel. When a hooked fish is coming toward us, or any time we need to retrieve the line quickly, the larger diameter will be appreciated. Usually, the smaller the spool diameter, the deeper the spool. This is necessary to make room for the fly line. On short rods intended for small brushy brooks and streams, a little reel can be fun, but its usefulness is limited.

Most fly reels are *single-action* reels. This means a one-to-one ratio: one winding of line for each revolution of the reel handle. How much line this amounts to per turn depends upon how big the diameter or core of line is on the reel. Remember, the larger the diameter, the quicker the line comes back onto the reel. This is the main advantage of a larger core diameter.

The use of backing will help increase the spool diameter and offers additional line in the event a big fish runs all the fly line off the reel. The average fly line is about ninety feet long, and while that is more than enough for light trout and panfish, it won't always be enough for strong fish in open water.

Backing is fine and strong, made either of Dacron or Micron. It is put on the empty reel first, and then the fly line is attached.

Palming an external-rim reel.

Twenty-pound test backing line is usually used for fresh water and thirty-pound for salt water. Almost all reels have room for some backing, and larger reels will often hold a couple hundred yards. A capacity chart from the reel manufacturer is usually included with its reel. Be sure to install just the right amount or you'll have a reel that is either too full or not full enough. Backing comes in different-sized spools just for this purpose.

Fly reels are available in both *internal* and *external rim*. On an external-rim model, the spool revolves on the outside of the reel. This way, you can "palm" the reel by letting it ride against the palm of your hand. This will help add tension in playing a bigger fish. This palming feature makes external-rim reels popular. Although seldom used on smaller fish, it's nice to know that palming can be used if a big fish comes along.

An internal-frame reel has a full frame that the spool slips into and no outside revolving spool. Internal-frame reels are a little heavier because of the extra framework, but they do provide additional protection to the spool should you drop the reel or fall and hit it on a rock.

Additional spools are available for most fly reels. These spools pop in and out of the reel just like a bobbin in a sewing machine. By using spare spools we can have different lines ready to fish. For instance, we may do most of our fishing with a floating line, but there might be one deep pool that we sometimes visit that is best fished with a sinking line. When we go to that pool, we will want to have our sinking line on a spare spool in a vest pocket. We can remove the spool with the floating line, insert the spool with the sinking line, and fish. Afterward, we can easily convert back to the floating line.

We seldom switch lines from pool to pool. We may fish a floating line with a sinking tip in the spring when the water is deep and fast and we want to fish underneath. Later on, we may fish the same water with a floating line.

When purchasing spare spools, a perfect fit is crucial. Whenever possible, take your reel along when shopping for a spool so you can try the fit. Even though spools appear to be identical, you'll sometimes find one that isn't quite right. Although spare spools are inexpensive and offer an easy way to switch lines, there is a definite downside. By having only one reel with spare spools, you must be very careful (or is it lucky?) that nothing happens to it. If you fall and break or damage the main frame of the reel, it may not work afterward. If this is your only reel, it could ruin a day or an entire trip. I like to keep several lines on various reels so I have a backup if I need one.

PERFORATED OR SOLID SPOOLS?

Fly reels can have either perforated or solid sides or a combination of both, with one side perforated and one solid. Years ago, perforation allowed air to circulate through the reel helping to dry the silk fly lines of the day. We don't need to worry about that with today's plastic-coated lines, but the perforations do reduce the reel weight somewhat and are aesthetically pleasing to most fishermen.

AUTOMATIC AND MULTIPLIER REELS

In addition to the popular single-action fly reels, also available are *multiplier* and *automatic* reels. Multiplier reels have an increased ratio for line retrieval. Instead of one-to-one, it may be one-and-a-half, or two-to-one—meaning that the line comes in much quicker. These are specific-use reels; they're a little heavier and have more parts.

Automatic reels have a lever that, when pressed, zips lengths of line back onto the reel. Although they once were thought of as pretty clever, they are too heavy, can easily break fine leaders, and are for the most part outdated.

FRESHWATER AND SALTWATER REELS

The main difference between a freshwater reel and a saltwater reel appears to be size; the larger and stronger the fish, the bigger the reel needs to be. That's true within each type of water as well. The small reel for brook trout will be inadequate for salmon or bass, even though all are caught in fresh water. It's also true that the reel that's ideal for bonefish will be inadequate for big tarpon,

A variety of fly reels.

both saltwater species. Most freshwater reels range from three to six ounces, and saltwater reels will always weigh more. In addition to size there are other differences, especially drag.

REEL MECHANICS

Drag systems are crucial in fly reels. Remember that the drag is the mechanical means for the reel to put pressure on the outgoing line; it also keeps the line from getting tangled when it's coming off the reel very fast. On average-sized trout and panfish reels, drag is not as important as it is with larger reels for fish like big trout, bass, and especially the larger and faster saltwater species.

The larger the fish, the larger the fly (generally) and the heavier the leader. Of course there are always exceptions, but this is true most of the time. Therefore, with a heavier, stronger leader, we can increase the tension on the outgoing line to help slow down and control the fish. We can't do this with a light leader because it would not be strong enough and would break and we'd loose the fish.

Basically, there are two types of drag: *spring and pawl* and *disk drag*. On small- to medium-sized freshwater reels a spring and pawl drag is adequate. This type of drag is easy to understand, hardly ever breaks, and is very popular. It consists of a toothed gear on the inside of the spool. When fitted into the frame, this gear engages the points of the pawl or pawls. Pressure is applied to the pawls by a double spring, also located on the inside of the frame. In turn, the pawls put tension on the toothed gear, which slows down the revolutions of the spool. Drag intensity is adjusted by a knob located on the outside of the frame.

Most of us get lazy with small fish and just strip the line in by hand once the fish is hooked, without using the reel at all. This is fine—with small fish. But don't let this habit carry over with larger fish. They are stronger and more unpredictable, and we need to have the line neatly stored on the reel when playing the fish in order to stay in control.

For bigger fish and heavier leaders, the disk drag provides smoother, more consistently, even tension for longer periods at high-revolution spool speeds. The simplest of the disk drags incorporates a cork or Teflon pad on the inside of the frame. This pad applies tension or pressure to stainless-steel disks. The spool locks down onto a pillar or stem in the frame and the drag is adjusted through a knob on the outside of the frame. Whether you choose spring and pawl or disk, most can usually be converted for the preferred retrieve—right- or left-hand.

Most modern saltwater reels have a disk-type drag and are either *direct drive* or *antireverse*. With a direct-drive reel, which is what most freshwater reels are, the reel handle revolves as the line goes out—or as a hooked fish is swimming away from us. A lesson easily learned the hard way is to keep our knuckles away from a fast-spinning reel handle.

An inside view of a spring-and-pawl reel drag mechanism (left), and a disk-drag mechanism (right).

With antireverse, the spool handle does not turn as the line is going out; the spool turns internally, independent of the handle. Antireverse reels are wonderful for big gamefish. With the heavier leaders used for this type of fishing, the angler can still reel in even as the fish is running line off the reel. And there are never any bruised knuckles.

Proper equipment is necessary to enjoy fly fishing, and these choices begin with the rod and reel we choose. If you're a new fly fisherman just getting started and you're going to fish mostly for trout and panfish, I'd recommend a medium-action eight- or eight-and-a-half-foot rod for a 5-weight line. This outfit will comfortably fish dry flies, wet flies, and streamers. After you've acquired some field experience, you may want to add a more specifically suited rod: perhaps a shorter rod for brushy situations, a slower-action rod for nymph fishing, or maybe a faster, longer rod for dry-fly fishing on a bigger river.

My first saltwater rod for bonefish and small tarpon was a Sage nine-foot rod for an 8-weight line, and it's still one of my favorites. I've added an nine-footer for a 9-weight for larger flies and windy days, and an 11-weight for bigger tarpon and permit.

My favorite freshwater reel for small to medium trout is a Lamson 1.5 reel. This reel is very well made, attractive looking, and balances well on my rod. For heavier trout, I have a Billy Pate antireverse trout model. I also have a Streamline and a Lamson 3.5.

For salt water, I have three favorites: two are Billy Pates and the other is a Lamson "Permit." For a less-expensive reel, I like the Scientific Anglers "Systems Two" reels in the appropriate size.

You should always buy the best gear you can afford. It's worth it in the end, and it's easier to enjoy fly fishing if you have good equipment.

3

USING THE GEAR

$\mathcal{S}$OME FISHERMEN CAN FIT ALL THEIR TACKLE and gear in a large duffle bag. Others need two large bags—one for gear and one for tackle. There are still others that need the two duffle bags plus the hall closet. Then there are those who need all of the above, plus a rod carrier and a tub (for wet boots) in the back of their four-wheel-drive (fishing car, which is gear, of course), plus a rod rack on the roof of the fishing car—and the spare bedroom, garage, and basement.

A large wet/dry bag partially packed for an outing, with wading shoes, waders, fly boxes, reel, hat, and belt.

Fly fishermen never give anything away. Just the thought "I might need this someday" is all it takes to move whatever "this"is to the back of the shelf or closet. I know for a fact that we have boxes of old stuff around our house that haven't been opened in years and years: old clippers, hats, leaders, fly line, spools that don't fit any of the reels we have, leaky boots, broken reels that haven't been repaired for years, and so on. That duffle may be just right to get started with, but don't throw it away when you've outgrown it. There will be something else to put in it—an old pair of leaky boots or something!

It is important to keep together all the things you need to take along when you go fishing. Necessary items are easily forgotten when scattered here and there throughout the house. There are great bags available that have dividers to separate the wet items from the dry. For a while, one of these bags will probably be able to carry everything you need. Let's look at what some of these things should be.

FISHING VEST, RAINCOAT, HAT, AND SUNGLASSES

It's fun to shop for a fishing vest. There are so many attractive colors and styles from which to choose. At one time, most vests were olive drab or tan. But today we have green greens, teals, tan with burgundy or teal trim; some women's vests even have plaid or paisley trim and linings. The vests are attractive and also functional.

When selecting a fishing vest, think about where you'll be

Ready to go with a well-fitted and functional fishing vest.

fishing most of the time. In the East, we have a lot of green foliage; in the West, we have big blue skies and prairies in addition to forests of spruce trees. It's important to blend in wherever you fish. This may be as simple as wearing a green shirt under your tan vest in the East and a light blue shirt under the same vest in the West. Stay away from wearing hot pinks, reds, whites, and other bright colors, because they can scare wary fish.

The length of the vest is also important. If it's too short, you won't have room for everything you may want to carry. But if it's too long, it will be in the water all the time and your flies will get wet and the hooks will rust. I am five feet four inches tall, and I like my vest to hang right at my belt. You should be able to get at least two 5³⁄₄-by-3³⁄₄-by-1¹⁄₄-inch boxes (a standard medium-sized fly box) in the front of the vest, along with one smaller box. Check this when you buy the vest—the same shop will have boxes you can try. There should also be a couple of smaller pockets on top of the larger pockets to hold split shot, strike indicators, lip balm, and other often-used small items.

On the inside of the vest there should be a lower pocket on

each side for varying-sized spools of leader/tippet material. You'll want room for at least four spools. A higher inside vertical pocket is ideal for sunglasses, insect repellent, or a small flashlight.

There should be at least one roomy pocket on the outside back of the vest for a lightweight raincoat, or a shirt for cool evenings or mosquitoes. A separate zippered pocket either on the back or inside the vest is a nice place to keep personal items like car keys.

Fishing vests are available in a variety of fabrics: cotton, cotton/polyester, mesh, Supplex, and so on. The mesh is especially nice in hot weather and when traveling light. I like the heavier cotton and cotton blends when I'm working out of a fully loaded vest—they don't ride up in the back. Sometimes, with the lighter vests, I find the back of my vest is up around my shoulder blades and the front is hanging in the water. Heavier fabric handles the weight distribution better. A knit collar is nice in a loaded vest—it doesn't cut into your neck during a long day.

Although most vests come with a front zipper, very few fishermen actually use this zipper. The pocket zippers are more important. Make sure they run smoothly. With a little practice, you should be able to get into the pockets with one hand.

A pin-on fleece or foam patch for keeping flies handy is standard issue with most vests. If the vest you've selected doesn't have one, buy it before you leave the store. If you have a choice, go with the foam patch. The foam doesn't disfigure wet flies as they dry—they stay hooked in better, and it's easier to get them out of the foam.

When you're trying on vests, keep in mind that as the pockets are filled, the vest will expand, making it feel smaller. Never buy a vest that is not loose and roomy. If it's too small to start with, it will only get smaller as you use it. A roomy vest will allow for warmer clothes in cold weather and will let the air flow through better in warm weather.

You'll find that some of the best fishing takes place in the rain. Insects often become very active and start hatching in light rain and drizzle. The fish will start sipping in these insects as they float on the water, and the fishing can be exciting. To enjoy fishing in these conditions, a good raincoat becomes a very important piece of gear.

Your fishing vest will stay dry if your raincoat is worn over it. A loaded fishing vest can be bulky, so the raincoat must be large enough to fit comfortably over the vest. There are lots of raincoats in different fabrics and price ranges that will do the job. You'll probably end up with two: one inexpensive lightweight nylon shell that can be stuffed in the back pocket of your vest for summer showers, and another, better, one to keep you dry in an all-day rain. The raincoat should be shorter than a nonrecreational rain-coat. It should be just long enough to completely cover your vest. Anything longer will hang in the water, and the pockets will fill with water. And sometimes, if the lining gets wet, the water will work its way up the inside of the jacket. You can imagine how comfortable a wet lining is!

Look for these features when shopping for a good raincoat: a storm flap over the zipper; a full-sized hood that fits over your cap; an O-ring sewn on the back for the net; hand-warmer pockets on the front; and adjustable cuffs of elastic, Velcro, or neoprene.

A good pair of sunglasses and a hat are more important today than ever before because of harmful ultraviolet rays. Make sure your sunglasses are polarized and provide UV protection. There are two primary lens colors: gray and amber. These two color groups include all the browns, tans, and greens. For bright, sunny days, most fishermen prefer a gray color. For overcast, cloudy, dark days, amber is best. Tan is a good choice for overall fishing conditions. Serious fishermen usually find themselves with a cou-ple pairs of sunglasses for different light conditions. If your eyes are sensitive to the light, or if you do a lot of fishing on bright, glar-ing flats or lakes, you may want to try a pair of side shields. Side shields provide additional protection and are sometimes included with the glasses, or they can be purchased separately.

On the average, women have smaller heads than men. Therefore, we often have trouble finding good polarized fishing glasses. There is one excellent fishing optics company that addresses this problem: Action-Optics, a division of Smith Sport Optics, in Ketchum, Idaho. I'm sure there are other companies, but I've used Action-Optics for years; the glasses are good, they don't slide down my nose, and they fit my small head.

A hat is another important piece of gear. Whether it's a base-ball cap, a visor, or any hat with a brim, it's necessary. A hat will provide additional protection from the sun, wind, and rain, and will help cut down the glare on bright days. A good hat combined with good sunglasses will allow you to see the fish better and quicker. Being able to see means you're going to get your fly there sooner, you'll be able to see the fish respond, and you'll thereby catch more fish. Try several designs and styles, and find one you like. Once you get used to wearing a hat, you'll wonder how you ever got along without it!

VEST ACCESSORIES

Pick up any good tackle catalog and you'll see a zillion things that you can carry in your vest. Obviously, some are more important than others, and what's useless to one fisherman may be priceless to the next. I've chosen to address what I think are the most important accessories, things I couldn't do without. Each of us will pick and choose as we become more experienced and as new products are introduced.

Basic saltwater accessories: from left *hook sharpener, saltwater fly, scissors, needle-nose pliers.*

My accessories don't change a lot from fresh to salt water. For the most part, salt water requires fewer accessories. A good pair of needle-nose pliers, a hook sharpener, and something to cut leader material with will just about do it—with a few flies.

For fresh water, my most important accessory hangs on the front of my vest on a retractor ("zinger"). It is a pair of Hardy three-inch scissor pliers. They are made by Hardy Brothers in England, the same people who make Hardy fly reels. There are lots of cheaper imitations, but the originals are the best. I use the scissor edge to cut leader material and to trim knots. The

Basic freshwater vest accessories: clockwise from left *split shot in canister, piece of cloth, fly floatant, chamois strip, scissor pliers on a retractor, strike indicators.*

pliers pinch on split shot, serve as a hook disgorger, and, with a little practice, can pinch down barbs. I use them continually while I'm fishing.

My fly floatant also hangs on the outside of my vest. I've used a silicone paste floatant for a number of years; it comes in a little plastic container with an attached lid and bead chain. I simply hook the bead chain through an O-ring on my vest. During cold weather I switch to a spray floatant because the paste gets too hard, but for most of my fishing I prefer the paste. Fly floatant is available in paste, spray, liquid, and powder crystals. They all work well. Again, it's personal choice.

To absorb all the water and fish slime from a dry fly, I keep a small piece of yellow chamois (about three by four inches) pinned inside my vest. Whenever a fly is not floating well, and always after releasing a fish, I wrap the chamois around the dry fly and squeeze out all the moisture. Then I apply the fly floatant and it's ready to fish again.

In a plastic thirty-five-millimeter film canister, I keep a variety of split shot in different sizes. I find this much easier than keeping track of numerous plastic tubes and self-locking bags. And with all the shot in one canister, I can easily find the right size. I pour them into the palm of my hand, pick out what I want, then put the rest back. It's also easy to see when I'm getting low on a certain size.

Strike indicators are in the pocket next to the split shot. I like the small round adhesive kind that wrap around the leader. They float well, cast easily, and are readily seen. The downside is that they are not adjustable or reusable. But they're inexpensive, and the used ones collect in a pocket until I can throw them away.

The last important small accessory to me is a piece of old tee shirt about eight inches square. It's folded up in a spare pocket and it gets used for all sorts of things. I wipe my hands on it, it's been a bandage in emergencies, it soaks up excess fly floatant and reel grease, and I wipe my brow and blow my nose on it, too! I have a couple and always keep a clean one on hand. I don't care if it gets lost or ruined, and I've come to rely on it.

Freshwater flies in a foam box.

To stay organized, keep all the small items in the same pockets all the time. If you do this, you'll always know which pocket to look in, and you'll save a lot of time not searching for something you know you have—somewhere!

You might only have one fly box in the beginning, but these too will multiply. Most fly boxes are plastic and have some kind of foam lining inside to hold the flies. The foam will be flat or ridged. The flat foam is designed for flies that can lie flat. The ridged foam is designed for flies that have hackle wrapped around their heads. The ridged-foam spaces protect the hackle from getting crushed. Be careful that your winged dry flies have enough depth in the box so that when you close the box the wings don't get damaged. With some boxes you'll want to arrange the flies so the wings don't collide when the box shuts. It's often a good idea to put flat flies all on one side and winged on the other so they're organized in the box. These are all tricks of the trade, and you'll discover the best ways to keep all your flies organized and safe.

You'll want to keep an extra leader in your vest somewhere. Only once have I had to replace a leader on the stream, but then I was glad to have one with me. A leader straightener is necessary

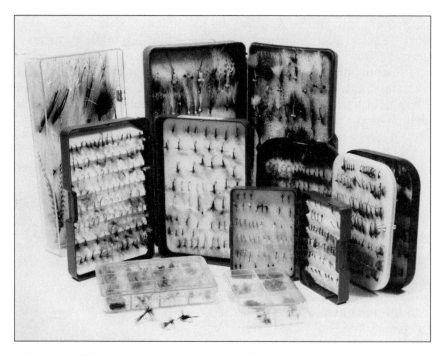

There is a fly box to suit every taste and pocket size.

unless your leader is flat monofilament (see chapter 4). The straightener consists of two small pads of rubber sewn together at the top. When the leader is pulled through the pads as they are being squeezed together, the friction and heat straightens stubborn monofilament that wants to re-coil. And of course, you'll have your extra spools of leader material in several sizes.

There are lots of extras that are either not always necessary, or that may be seasonal: a light by which to change flies after dark or to help you find your way back to the car, a stream thermometer if you're into recording and checking water temperatures, a magnifier if you have trouble with those tiny flies, a hook sharpener (more important in salt water), boot patch, sunscreen, and so on.

LANDING NET

There is a lot of controversy about landing nets. Some believe a net should not be used at all; others think one should always be used—and back and forth it goes.

When I fish in salt water with a guide and boat, I let the guide decide. If he wants to use a big net and bring the fish in the boat, he's calling the shots, and I do what I can to assist. When I'm wading the flats alone, I don't use a net. I'm usually fishing for bonefish or permit, and with a pair of needle-nose pliers, I can easily remove the hook and release the fish.

In Alaska and similar places, when I'm fishing for big fish (say, over four pounds) in very cold water, I don't use a net. The leader is generally strong enough to land the fish before it's exhausted, and most landing nets are too small. Again, I use a pair of pliers and quickly release the fish—and it recovers instantly. I think getting the fish off the hook and back into the water quickly is important. I've never seen a fish in any of these instances that wasn't ready to take off as soon as it was free.

However, when I am fishing in the States, both in the East and the West, I always use a net for trout over ten inches. I seldom use a net for panfish, perch, or bass; however, I have for bass on the river because it's easier to work with them in the net in the current there, especially because they are not played out. Perch and panfish can be landed easily, are more tolerant of being handled, and recover quickly.

Trout are more sensitive and delicate. They bruise easily, and in warm summer water temperatures become exhausted. It's easy to unintentionally injure a trout internally. By using a net and keeping the fish in the water, I can release it much quicker than if it's flopping around on the bank or the edge of the stream with me frantically grabbing it. I can gently hold the fish through the net with my left hand while removing the hook with my right. If it is being difficult, sometimes turning it belly-up will calm it. Then, with the fish upright in the net in the water, it can be released and will swim away from the net.

Trout should always be released in slower water, facing upstream. If the fish is played out from a long hard fight, gently cradle it in the water, allowing it to rest on the palms of your hands. Provide just enough support so that it can swim out of your hands when it's ready.

Fish will recover quicker in cold water. If the surface of the water feels warmer than the deeper water, hold the fish deeper, or take a couple of steps out to colder water. Never release a tired trout in fast current or before it's ready—it may not have the strength to recover.

Choose a net with a black cotton bag rather than a green or

light-color nylon. The cotton will be softer when wet, and the dark color won't frighten the fish. Hold the net in the water as you bring the fish to the net. This will give the cotton a chance to get wet, and keeping the bag in the water won't startle the fish.

WADING GEAR

Women are fortunate today because we have lots of fabrics, sizes, and styles of waders to choose from. Manufacturers are making good waders specifically for women. Until recently, we had to make do with boys' or men's waders, and most of the time they were uncomfortable, often being too big in the feet, around the middle, in the length, or all of the above. Often, when we got them to fit in one place, another place wouldn't fit at all. Waders were a disaster for us all the way around!

Chest waders fit up to just under the armpits and are held up with suspenders. *Waist waders* are usually neoprene and fit like a pair of jeans—to the waist, and they stay up by themselves. *Hip boots* cover most of the leg, like a pair of chaps with feet, and are held up by loops that attach around belts or belt loops. Chest waders and hip boots are the most common and easily found forms of waders made for women.

Hip boots are great for hot summer days on small streams, places that are shallow and easy to wade. Chest waders are more practical for medium to large streams and rivers. You'll be able to move around more freely, and they are warmer and drier during wet cold weather.

Waders and hip boots are available in a number of fabrics. For cold weather and cold water, neoprene is the best material. Neoprene is the material used in scuba-diving suits, and it is very warm and stretches, which makes it easy to move around in. It is available in different thicknesses, from two- to five-millimeter, with three-millimeter the most popular thickness. It is easy to clean and patch.

For warmer-weather fishing, a pair of lightweight waders are fine. Lightweights are often chosen because a layer of fleece or warmer layered clothes can be added under the waders. As the weather gets warmer, those underlayers can be eliminated. The most common lightweight fabrics are Supplex, nylon, and Gore-tex.

Once you decide on the fabric, you must then decide

A landing net in use. It's obviously important to keep the line tight throughout the landing process.

whether to buy either stocking-foot or boot-foot style. "Stocking foot" simply means that a boot is not attached and must be purchased separately.

Wading shoes, or boots, are available in different materials and designs to fit over the stocking foot on the wader or hip boot. The most popular is a Cordura or synthetic leather lacing boot. The synthetic leather is lightweight, doesn't rot or mildew, dries quickly, and is maintenance-free. The lace-up style provides excellent support and provides stability while wading.

"Boot foot" means that the boot is attached to and thus part of the wader. You put your feet into the boots and pull up the rest of the wader. Boot-foot waders are much quicker to get in and out of and eliminate the need for a wading shoe. They are also much warmer because of the extra room in the boot, where extra socks can usually be worn. However, this style doesn't provide the support that wading shoes do, and you can feel clumsy in it. If you're doing a lot of walking, wading shoes are best. With one pair of properly sized wading shoes, you can wear either light-

Neoprene waders and wading shoes (left) and lightweight boot-foot waders (right).

weight or neoprene stocking-foot waders. You may need an extra pair of socks with the lightweights, but you can actually have two complete systems with one pair of shoes. You can even add a pair of stocking-foot hip boots to the same system.

Most boot-foot waders and wading shoes have felt soles. The felt will grab slippery rocks and stream bottoms, providing better traction than the old rubber lug soles. However, in mud lug soles are better. For most fishing situations felt will be best—it's easy to take care of and can be replaced when necessary.

When you're buying waders, don't forget suspenders. They are usually built into neoprene and Gore-tex waders but may have to be purchased separately for the other fabrics.

And before leaving the store, buy a wading belt. This is usually a nylon or neoprene belt with a plastic quick-release that is worn on the outside of light-weight waders. If you should fall in the water without a wading belt, the waders can quickly fill up with water, making it impossible for you to get out. This simple belt can actually save your life and should be worn at all times with loose-fitting waders. When I take my belt off, I hook it through the suspenders on my waders, insuring that it will always be handy and ready to wear.

Everything you need for safe, comfortable wading: clockwise from left *wading socks, wading shoes, and gravel guards.*

If you're buying lightweight stocking-foot waders, you may want to add a pair of neoprene wading socks or gravel guards. If your lightweight waders have a neoprene foot, then you'll only need a pair of gravel guards, which fit around the top of your wading shoes to keep grit and gravel from washing down inside. If there is no neoprene foot on the waders, consider a pair of neoprene wading socks. These socks go on over the stocking-foot waders before the wading shoe. They often have a built-in cuff that is pulled down over the top of the shoe after being laced. This cuff keeps out grit and gravel. Never put a nylon, Supplex, or Gore-tex stocking foot directly inside a wading shoe. A sock between the stocking foot and the shoe will help prevent grit from wearing holes into the fabric of the wader. A sock will also help cushion the foot.

A wading staff is another important piece of gear, especially when you're wading in unfamiliar water, water that is not clear, or in fast water. If you can't see into the water, you won't see holes, ledges, boulders, or slippery rocks. A wading staff will help you probe ahead to locate these problem areas.

In fast current, a staff can provide additional support and will act like a third leg to help you wade through. For obvious reasons, if the current is strong and doesn't feel safe, don't try it. Look for a better place to cross, perhaps where the river is wider and shallower. I've often looked for a good stout stick on the stream bank to help me get through strange water. Whether you have a manufactured wading staff or a heavy stick, it can make a big difference in touchy situations.

There are collapsible staffs available that conveniently fold up to go in a pouch worn on your belt. If you use a conventional one-piece staff, keep it on your downstream side so it doesn't get tangled up in your legs. It can be attached to your wading belt and should stay out of the way until you need to reach for it.

HELPFUL LISTS

NECESSARY ACCESSORIES

Wet/dry bag

Fishing vest

Hat

Sunglasses

Retractors (or "zingers")

Scissor pliers

Fly floatant

Chamois

Split shot

Strike indicators

Piece of cloth

Fly boxes

Extra leader

Leader straightener

Landing net

WADING GEAR

Waders

Wading shoes (for stocking-
    foot waders)

Wading socks (for lightweight
    waders)

Wading staff

Belt

Suspenders

Raincoat

EXTRAS

Small light

Stream thermometer

Magnifier

Hook sharpener

Boot patch

Sunscreen

SALTWATER

Fly boxes

Extra leader

Needle-nose pliers

Snip-to-cut leader

Hook sharpener

Piece of cloth

Sunscreen

4

LINES, LEADERS, and KNOTS

I F YOU'VE EVER STOOD IN A FLY SHOP AS A nonfisherman in front of a display of fly lines and leaders, you know firsthand how confusing and intimidating all this can be. But by working patiently through this chapter you will see that lines and leaders are not only extremely important but also quite understandable.

FLY LINES

All modern fly lines consist of a level, braided core material coated with a plastic finish. Varying thicknesses of the

Relationship between fish, line size and hook (fly) size.

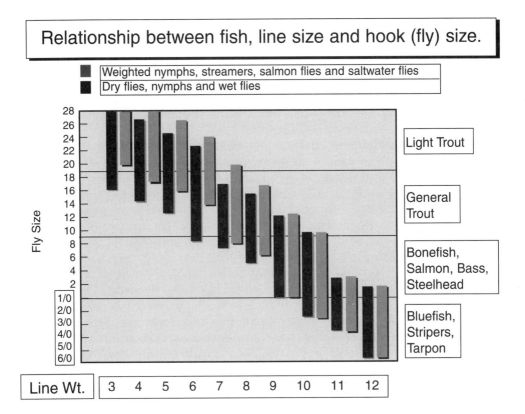

Legend:
- Weighted nymphs, streamers, salmon flies and saltwater flies
- Dry flies, nymphs and wet flies

Fly Size (vertical axis): 28, 26, 24, 22, 20, 18, 16, 14, 12, 10, 8, 6, 4, 2, 1/0, 2/0, 3/0, 4/0, 5/0, 6/0

Right labels: Light Trout; General Trout; Bonefish, Salmon, Bass, Steelhead; Bluefish, Stripers, Tarpon

Line Wt.: 3 4 5 6 7 8 9 10 11 12

plastic coating gives us a taper: *weight-forward, double taper, triangle taper*, and *level*. The finish on the line makes different functions possible: *floating, sinking, intermediate sinking*, and *sinking tip*.

In chapter 2, we learned that all rods have a recommended line size and that buying the correct size is as easy as following the rod manufacturer's suggestion. To get the best performance out of your rod and line, it's important that the two match. If the line is too light, it cannot load or flex the rod. On the other hand, if the line is too heavy, the rod will not be strong enough to handle it. As lines increase in weight, the matching rods will increase in weight and strength. Since the line is heavier, the leader and tippet will also be heavier. Heavier lines usually mean bigger flies, and a stronger leader is needed to turn over these flies.

Most fly lines are about ninety feet in length. The line size is determined by the weight in grains of the first thirty feet, regardless of taper or function. The next step is understanding line function and taper.

FUNCTION

Most fly fishermen most of the time use a floating line. Because they float, these lines are easy to cast and easy to see. Most fly fishermen enjoy using a floating line and fishing with dry flies (flies that float) because the flies are weightless, easy to cast, and fun to watch. But there are times when the fish are not near the surface and you must use flies that sink.

A monofilament leader is necessary on the end of the fly line to complete the cast. This piece of monofilament is attached to the fly line, and the fly is attached to the other end of the leader. Without the leader, the fly line would land hard on the water, scaring the fish. Also without the leader, the fly would have to be tied to the end of the fly line, which is impossible: the fly line is thicker than the diameter of some of the eyes on small hooks.

To make a fly sink with a floating line, lead weight can be attached to the leader in various forms, such as split shot, lead putty, or lead sleeves. As the leader sinks, the fly sinks. You can also use a weighted fly, which has lead wrapped on the hook before the fly is tied. To get more depth, the leader can be lengthened, more weight can be added, or both methods can be used.

If you find that a floating line is not getting the fly deep enough, you may need a line that sinks. A good choice might be a sinking-tip line because it is not too difficult to cast and most of the line floats, making lifting the line off the water easier. The sinking-tip portion is available in different lengths, most commonly from four to fifteen feet, and in different sink rates. The sink rate is determined by how many inches per second (ips) the line will sink. Most of these lines sink anywhere from 1½ ips to 6 ips, depending on specific fishing requirements. For deep fast-

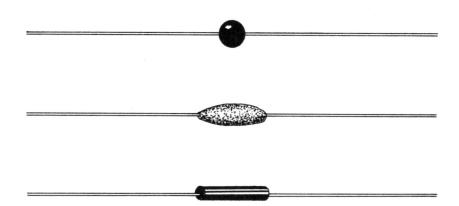

Different ways of weighting the leader: split shot (top), lead putty (middle), and lead sleeve (bottom).

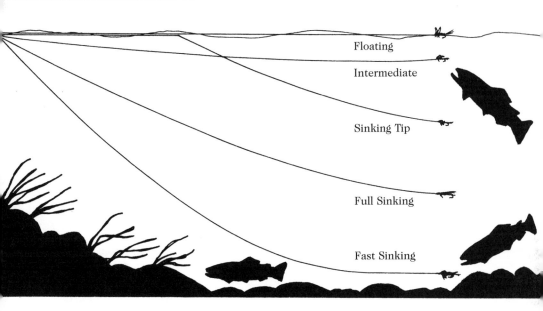

Floating

Intermediate

Sinking Tip

Full Sinking

Fast Sinking

Various line types and the depths to which they sink.

moving water a higher ips rate will be needed to get the fly down to where the fish are, but this line may get hung up on the bottom in slower water where the current is not as strong.

A full-sinking or an intermediate line are two other options. To achieve maximum depth, or for trolling, a sinking line may be the answer. These lines sink very quickly but are difficult to cast. The casting loop should be opened up (see chapter 5) so the turn-around from backcast to forward cast is slowed down. If the turn-around is made too quickly, it shocks the cast and makes a smooth delivery impossible. The line travels fast because of the narrow profile, and positioning your cast out away from your shoulder a couple of extra inches will keep the line well away from your head. Sinking lines are difficult to pick up from the water, and retrieving a good portion of the line is often necessary before making a new cast.

An intermediate line is slightly denser than water and stays just below the surface. These lines are easier to cast than are full-sinking lines and are often used in weedy lakes and ponds because the line doesn't descend as deep as a sinking line. For this reason, they are also easier to pick up from the water to cast.

A fairly new product is the mini-sinking tip, or lead head. These are shorter lengths of sinking line, usually twelve to thirty inches, that can be attached to the front of a floating line. Mini-sinking tips are easy to attach and remove, economical, available in different densities, and can be carried easily in a vest pocket. In about a minute you can turn your floating line into a sinking tip without switching lines.

TAPER

Taper is determined by the density of the plastic coating on the fly line. Usually, most of the weight of the fly line is found in the first thirty to forty feet. As the taper varies from short to long and thick to thin, the results show up in differences in the way the line feels on the rod and in the presentation.

The most-often-used taper is the weight-forward. Behind the first thirty to forty feet of a weight-forward line is thinner line called *running line*. The leader can be attached easily to the front taper and a delicate presentation achieved. Although weight-forward lines were first developed for distance casting, they are the easiest lines to cast in any situation because of the weight in the front taper.

The double taper has an identical taper at each end. Instead of having the weight concentrated in the forward section of the line, it continues back through the line until it tapers again at the other end. This line is popular because it can be turned around after an end wears out, resulting in a new front taper. Although

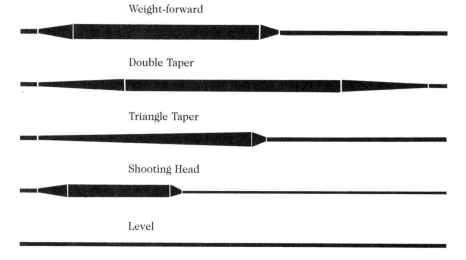

Weight-forward

Double Taper

Triangle Taper

Shooting Head

Level

The various tapers of fly line.

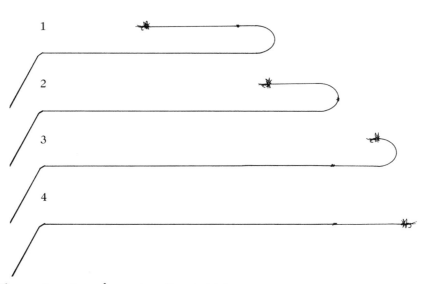

The progression of a cast as it opens up.

some experienced anglers prefer the double taper, especially for long, delicate casts, the taper on the weight-forward is still easier for new fishermen.

The triangle taper was developed by the late Lee Wulff and is a modification of the weight-forward. The longer front taper and thick middle (or belly) makes it a good line for roll casting (see chapter 5) without sacrificing a delicate presentation. This particular line encompasses two line sizes. A 4/5, for instance, can be used equally well on a 4- or 5-weight rod. It will cast better short on the 4-weight and better on the 5-weight with longer casts.

A *shooting head* is a short, heavy front taper (usually thirty feet) with thin running line behind. Sometimes this running line is monofilament. Shooting heads were developed for steelhead fishermen who need to make long casts quickly, often into fast water. The monofilament running line reduces weight and surface friction as the line travels through the guides. Very fast line speeds and greater distances are easily achieved, but delicate presentations on the water are impossible. Shooting heads are available in all functions, from floating to extra-fast-sinking, and in all sizes.

The level line is not a taper at all but a level consistent diameter from one end of the line to the other. Level lines are inexpensive to manufacture and to sell, but don't be fooled by the price. They are difficult to cast because there is no forward taper

There is a lot of information on a fly-line box. Note the taper prefixes, line-size numbers, and line functions.

to help load or bend the rod, and attaching a leader is difficult because the thick fly line is impossible to work into a small knot. Delicate presentations on the water are difficult; you'll scare the fish and have trouble casting. So do yourself a favor and buy a weight-forward.

There are other specialty tapers: bass bug, bonefish, spring creek, and so on. Most of these are modifications of a weight-forward with variations in the forward taper to promote ease in casting big flies, handling wind, or getting a softer presentation. In the beginning, if you learn the tapers described here, you'll know the most important ones and won't be confused.

Taper, line weight, and function are all indicated on the fly-line box. The taper is indicated by the prefix on most boxes: WF is for weight-forward, DT for double taper, TT for triangle taper. The number in the middle indicates the line weight, which corresponds to the rod. And the last letter or letters tell us the function of the line: F for floating, F/S for float sink (sinking tip), S for sinking. (See the photograph above.)

FLY-LINE COLOR

Much has been written about the color of fly lines. There was a time when all lines were dark green, brown, or gray. Today we have light colors to choose from: yellow, light green, tan, ivory, and even orange.

There are distinct advantages to using bright lines. When you're getting started it's important to watch your cast, especially when you're practicing casting. A light-colored fly line is much easier to see and watch in the air. It's also easier to locate on the water. There will often be times when you can't see your dry fly, and by finding the end of the fly line and judging the distance for the leader, you can determine about where your fly is drifting. And sometimes you can detect when a fish has taken your fly underwater by watching as the end of the fly line moves forward in the water a few inches.

These are reasons enough for me to use bright lines. I don't think they scare the fish more than other lines. Our false casts should be behind the fish anyway, and our leader long enough so the cast doesn't startle them. I firmly believe that presentation is far more important than line color.

FLY-LINE MAINTENANCE

If you find that your floating line is beginning to sink or is not casting well, it may need to be cleaned. All lines benefit from being clean. There are excellent fly-line cleaners available, but it's hard to beat Armor All. Yes, the same Armor All that is used on car interiors and tires.

To clean or dress your line, cast as much line as you can onto your lawn and then pull off another ten feet and lay the rod down. Take a paper towel and make a wet spot of Armor All in it. Start at the tip of the rod, fold the wet area of the paper towel around the line, and pull the line through as you walk toward the leader. Run the leader through, too, then fold the towel to a clean, dry spot and pull the line through it as you walk back toward the rod.

You'll be amazed at how much easier a clean line will cast. Line cleaner is just like furniture polish is to fine wood—it puts a clean, slippery finish on the fly line. A clean fly line will float better and will be easier to cast.

Beware of insect repellents containing DEET (di-ethyl-toluamide). DEET is very harmful to any plastic surface—fly lines, boxes, sunglasses—and is easily transferred to the line from your hands. The result will be a dry, cracked fly line that must eventually be replaced.

There was a time, and not too many years ago, when fly lines were not the fine tools they are today. Before the advent of nylon and plastic (pre-WWII), lines were made of silk and required careful handling and a lot of maintenance. The lines were sized by diameter, and finding the perfect line for a particular rod was not an easy task. We are fortunate, because today's lines require little care, perform well, and are available in many different tapers, sizes, functions, and colors.

LEADERS

In order to make consistently good casts, we must pay attention to our leader. This simple piece of monofilament can determine where the fly lands, how it behaves on or in the water, whether it is accepted or rejected by the fish, and, sometimes, whether we land or lose the fish.

The energy from our casting arm is transmitted through the rod into the fly line, leader, and on into the fly. The hopeful end result is the fly landing on the water ahead of the leader with just the right amount of slack to allow it to behave like a natural insect. If there is too much slack, the leader cannot straighten out, the cast collapses, and the fly falls back on the leader or off to the side. Without enough slack, the fly will land hard and drag. When there is drag or tension on the fly, it will look like it's being pulled along or attached to something. Any self-respecting fish will refuse both casts.

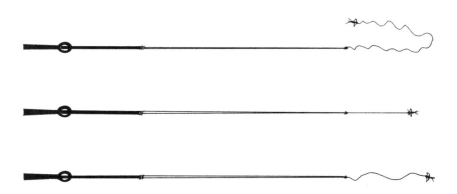

A leader can turn over in various ways: too long (top), too short (middle), just right (bottom).

Basic leader function is the same in fresh and salt water. However, saltwater conditions often require certain leader changes, and these are discussed in chapter 11.

Leaders are made of monofilament, which is nylon, and decrease in diameter from a heavy end to a light end. When the fish takes our fly, we *strike* to *set the hook*. Since nylon stretches, the leader will stretch just enough to soften the strike so we don't break the leader and lose the fish. Of course, it's easy to strike too hard or too soft, resulting in either a lost fish or no hook-up.

LEADER FORMULA

The heavy end of the leader is the *butt section*, which is followed by a *midsection* and finally the *tippet*. The taper can be achieved by using a hand-tied leader or a knotless tapered leader. Hand-knotted leaders consist of up to ten sections of monofilament tied together, starting with the heaviest and ending with the lightest, or the tippet. Knotless tapered leaders are extruded through a

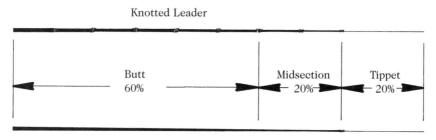

A comparison of a knotted and a knotless leader with attached tippet sections, and the percentages of the decreasing diameters.

manufacturing process resulting in various lengths and tippet strengths. The standard leader, whether knotted or knotless, consists of about 60 percent butt section, 20 percent midsection, and 20 percent tippet.

Leaders are tapered for two reasons. First, the butt section has to be thick enough to be attached to the end of the fly line so the energy of the cast can pass smoothly from the fly line to the leader. And second, the tippet must be compatible with the anticipated hook size. As the hook size decreases, so must the tippet size. The energy of the cast is continuously transmitted by heavier line turning over lighter line until the fly lands delicately at the end of the cast.

The tippet section should be at least twenty-four inches long to allow enough slack for the fly to act naturally and to allow for a number of changes before it must be replaced.

In order to fully understand today's leaders, we should first look back to the pre-nylon leaders. In his book, *The New American Trout Fishing*, John Merwin writes about leaders:

> The silkworm-gut leaders in wide use from about the 1880s to the 1950s are difficult to visualize in this age of synthetics. These weren't really gut, as being derived from the worm's stomach or intestine, but were made from the worm's silk glands. Each gland and its contents were hand stretched and drawn through a series of dies and then allowed to air dry as stiff filament as much as two feet long. The drawing process gave rise to the "X" system of leader diameter measurement; for example, a 4X gut strand was drawn through four successive dies to a reasonably consistent diameter of about .007-inch. Gut strands were relatively short and had to be knotted together to make a leader of reasonable length, with heavy strands at one end to mate with the stiffness and diameter of the fly line point and fine strands at the other end to ensure a delicate delivery of the fly.

It is this "X" system that we still use today to measure and label leaders. You can easily understand this system by studying the accompanying chart. Let's take the 4X leader Mr. Merwin uses in his description, for example. The designation of 4X, which is .007-inch in diameter, is compatible with hook sizes 12, 14, and 16, and is approximately 5.5-pound test. Regardless of the brand of leader you buy, the X size and the diameter will always be consistent. In other words, every 4X leader will be .007-inch in diameter. It is the pound test that sometimes varies slightly between brands. It is important to have the strongest, finest leader available, and once I find one I like, I stay with that brand.

MEASURE AND LABEL LEADERS

Tippet Sizes	Diameter (in inches)	Balances with Fly sizes	Approximate Pound Test
0X	.011	2, 1/0	12.0
1X	.010	4, 6, 8	10.0
2X	.009	6, 8, 10	9.0
3X	.008	10, 12, 14	7.0
4X	.007	12, 14, 16	5.5
5X	.006	14, 16, 18	4.0
6X	.005	16, 18, 20, 22	3.0
7X	.004	18, 20, 22, 24	2.0
8X	.003	22, 24, 26, 28	.75

LEADERS AND TIPPETS

Leaders are always sold by the tippet size and length. Sometimes the package will also give the butt diameter, but a 4X leader always indicates a 4X tippet size. Since the most common leaders are seven, nine, and twelve feet, and the most commonly used freshwater hooks are 12, 14, and 16, a nine-foot 4X leader is very popular. As the chart indicates, there is a little overlap from hook size to tippet size. A size 14 hook can be used with 3X, 4X, or 5X. A big, bushy, heavy #14 fly will turn over better on 3X, which will be a little stiffer, and a lightly dressed, delicate #14 might be fine on 5X. This also leaves a little room for error on our part. But if the tippet is too heavy for the fly, the fly will drag and not look natural. If it is too light, the tippet will not be able to turn over during the cast and the fly will collapse in a puddle of monofilament at the end. If this happens, the tippet simply needs to be adjusted to better match the fly. When fishing over fussy fish, a longer tippet is almost always an advantage because there is less drag on the fly and the finer tippet isn't as likely to frighten the fish.

Tippet or leader material is available on small spools in all X sizes and heavier. These spools can be carried in your fishing vest for replacing tippets and are also used for building hand-tied knotted leaders. The chart above goes from 0X to 8X, which are the most common tippet sizes used in fresh water.

The X system doesn't go beyond 0X, so for tippet sizes heavier than 0X (.011-inch), we simply use the diameter and the pound test. Tippet for salmon or big bass might be .017-inch or fifteen-pound test. We would also be able to fish larger flies on these larger diameters of tippet.

The tippet on a knotless leader may simply be the level extruded end of the long taper, or it may be a piece of level monofilament tied to the end of the taper. Most tippet sections will average in length from fifteen to twenty-four inches. I prefer a separate, attached tippet for a couple of reasons. First of all, every time you change flies or get stuck on the bottom or in a tree, the tippet section gets a little shorter. If the tippet is attached, you can easily see how much you have left, and thus will know when it's time to replace the tippet section. Because the taper is not affected, the tippet diameter will be compatible with the taper. And, if your tippet is 4X and you want to fish a #20 fly, you can easily shorten the 4X to about ten inches and add twenty-four inches of 6X. On the

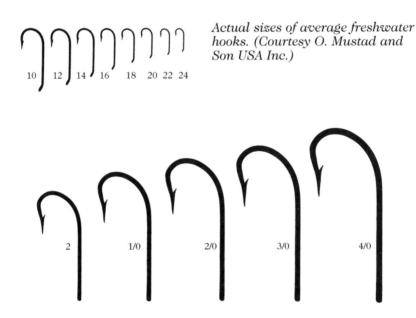

Actual sizes of average freshwater hooks. (Courtesy O. Mustad and Son USA Inc.)

10   12   14   16   18   20   22   24

2   1/0   2/0   3/0   4/0

Actual sizes of average saltwater hooks. (Courtesy O. Mustad and Son USA Inc.)

Assorted packages and spools of leader material.

other hand, if you want to fish 4X, simply cut off the 6X and the 4X and reattach twenty-four inches of new 4X. Don't attach 4X to 4X when you can eliminate a knot by replacing it completely.

Most monofilament is compatible in .002-inch increments. There are a couple of hard monofilaments, Mason for instance, that are not compatible with more commonly used brands, but most can be mixed with one another. A diameter of .005-inch (6X) is compatible with .007-inch (4X), and .007-inch is compatible with .009-inch (2X), and so on. A diameter of .007 inches would not be compatible with .003 inches (8X). The knot wouldn't hold and would create a weak spot in the leader, probably breaking when you hooked a fish. It would also interrupt the smooth transfer of energy, and the leader would not turn over well. The leader would kick off to the side and be very frustrating to work with.

Because a little bit of the leader is used up every time you attach a new tippet section, eventually you will need to add a new piece of monofilament to replace what's been used. The diameter of this new section needs to be compatible with both the end of the remaining leader and the tippet. Now you will have two knots in your leader, one attaching the new midsection and one for the tippet. If you always have a spool of 2X, 4X, 5X, and 6X in your vest, you can make most of the needed adjustments to your fresh-water trout leader. You won't need the 5X and the 6X for panfish and bass.

Always keep your leaders and spools of leader material in your fishing vest, closet, or gear bag. Don't store this material where it is exposed to light. The monofilament can deteriorate and weaken in light. It's a good idea to throw away old spools at the beginning of the year and replace them with fresh stock, especially in the smaller diameters.

As with lines, you will see specialty leaders for bass, saltwater, spring creek, and other applications. These leaders may have heavier butts for turning over bigger flies or longer front tapers for delicate turnovers with tiny flies and long tippets. They are designed for specific fishing situations, and in the beginning the differences will be hardly noticeable to the inexperienced fly fisherman.

LEADER COLOR

Most leaders are clear, brown, or a shade of green in order to be camouflaged in the water. Fish have excellent eyesight, and how effective leader color actually is in fooling the fish is debatable. Fish live in a world where objects are always drifting past: sticks, debris, stems, and leaves. So things passing through their territory is quite normal; however, anything moving and looking alive may pose a threat to the fish. Never hastily pick up a cast when the leader is over or near a fish.

Leaders are available with dyed fluorescent butt sections. These aid the fishermen in locating the fly, and I've used them with much success. Since most freshwater leaders are seven to twelve feet long, it's easy to have three or four feet of fluorescent butt with the rest of the leader clear.

FLAT-BUTT LEADERS

Most leaders are made with round monofilament, which has "memory"—the leader will retain coils after being taken out of the package and can look like a slinky on the water. Sometimes stretching the leader or pulling it through a leader straightener or piece of rubber or leather to create heat and friction will help eliminate these frustrating coils.

Another solution is to use flat-butt leaders. Flat monofilament doesn't retain memory. It straightens easily by being stretched and turns over straight because of the flat profile. I first used flat-butt leaders about ten years ago. They are still my favorite freshwater leader and are marketed by Doug Swisher in Hamilton, Montana. They are available in clear or dyed butt with a clear tippet attached. The dyed butt section makes locating your fly easier on the water.

BRAIDED LEADERS

Braided nylon leaders are strands of supple monofilament braided together. They have no memory and stretch to protect fine tippets. However, I have seen silt from streams clog the braid, sinking the leader, and the spray that comes off the leader when casting can scare the fish. My advice is to try them and make your own decision.

KNOTS

It's important to know a few knots that you are comfortable tying. Some knots, like the surgeon's knot and the clinch knot, will be used often. Others, like the arbor knot and the nail knot, are used less often and can usually be tied at home instead of on the stream. The shoelace knot is great for wading shoes and for teaching children because it's easy and won't work loose. An sooner or later you'll have to tie up a boat, and the interlocking knot will then come in handy. Included here are a few saltwater knots, including the nonslip mono loop and the haywire twist, and the interlocking knot for loop-to-loop connections.

The knots in this chapter are taken from *Practical Fishing Knots*, by Mark Sosin and Lefty Kreh, an excellent guide to all kinds of knots and well worth having in your book collection.

The authors give us some sound knot advice, such as wetting the knot before pulling it tight with either water or saliva, and using pliers with heavy monofilament, which can easily slip or cut. It's important to follow the directions carefully. Don't assume you can go in from the back when the directions tell you to go in from the front—it can make a big difference!

Knots are either a blessing or a curse. They can be the difference between getting a fish or losing it. Wind knots are caused by poor casting and tangle the leader. Each wind knot is a weak spot that can break when you're fighting a fish. But good knots are necessary, and if properly tied won't hinder your chances at landing a big fish.

Practice your knots and become comfortable with them. It's a great feeling to land fish and to know your properly tied knots made it possible.

◆ SURGEON'S KNOT ◆

The surgeon's knot is used to attach two lengths of monofilament of different diameters. It is not recommended for monofilament over sixty-pound test, because it can not be drawn tight with hand pressure. When tied properly, the surgeon's knot approaches one hundred percent efficiency. It can be tied in the dark, and it's easy.

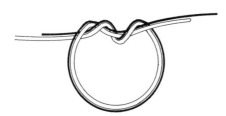

STEP 1: The end from the reel should come in from the left and the piece you're attaching should come in from the right. Let the two overlap about eight inches (when you are more practiced, you can use less overlap).

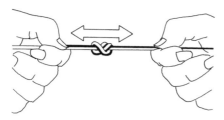

Surgeon' knot

STEP 2: Squeezing the part that overlaps with the thumb and forefinger of both hands, make a loop by going around a couple of fingers on your left hand with the overlapped line.

STEP 3: Take your fingers out of the loop and pass the long and the short ends on the right side completely through the loop twice.

STEP 4: Pull the loop closed by taking the long and the short ends on the left and on the right and pulling. Make sure you have both lines in each hand, and moisten the knot before tightening it.

STEP 5: Pull individual strands if the knot is not tight, and trim the short ends.

◆ CLINCH KNOT ◆

This is a simple knot for attaching flies to a leader of up to twelve-pound test. This knot is effective in freshwater fishing for trout, panfish, and light bass. For tippets over twelve pounds, use the nonslip mono loop knot.

STEP 1: Put at least six inches of material through the eye of the fly and double it back on the leader.

STEP 2: Wrap the end that went through the eye around the standing line six times for leaders less than eight pounds and four times for eight pounds and above.

Clinch knot

STEP 3: Pass the end through the small loop that has formed at the eye of the hook. Hold the end flush against the fly and pull gently with the other hand. You will see the wraps slide down against the eye of the fly. Moisten the knot as the wraps start to slide.

STEP 4: Tug on the fly, and when you're sure it's not going to slip further, trim the end close to the knot.

◆ TIE-FAST NAIL KNOT ◆

This knot is illustrated with a Tie-Fast Knot Tyer tool. This tool, or a similar version, can be found in most tackle shops. The nail knot is used whenever fly line is involved. Most of the time, this is when either the backing or the leader is attached to the fly line.

STEP 1: Place the leader or backing in the tool channel, with about six inches hanging out the front of the tool. Place the thumb of the tool-holding hand on top of the line. With the other hand, take hold of the six inches and, pulling down and counterclockwise up around the end of the tool, make five wraps, one next to the other, working back to the left. Tension must be applied constantly while wrapping or the slack will cause the wraps to slide off the tool.

STEP 2: As soon as the fifth wrap is completed, put the forefinger of your tool-holding hand on the back of the wraps to hold them in place. With the other hand, take the loose end and pass it under the wraps, moving from the back to the front of the tool. Pull it all the way through.

STEP 3: Take the end of the fly line and pass it from front to back under the wraps. Work it through until it, too, is lying up on top next to the other line. Continue to maintain pressure with your forefinger on the wraps.

STEP 4: While applying pressure to both lines with the thumb

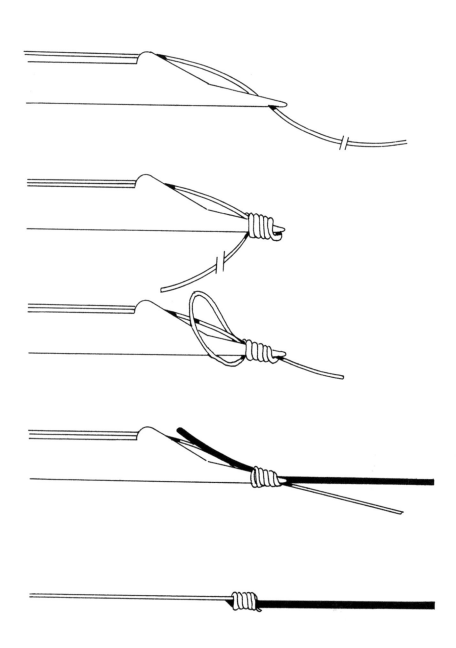

Tie-fast nail knot

of your tool-holding hand, take hold of the short end hanging out in front of the tool and quickly pull it and the knot off the end of the tool. Before pulling tight to finish the knot, the wraps can be adjusted with your thumbnail and the knot can be pushed down to the end of the fly line to avoid waste.

STEP 5:   Give the knot a few good tugs with the long end of the fly line and the long end of the other line to make sure it's tight. Trim the short ends. If desired, you can add a drop of rubber-based cement to the knot so it goes in and out of the fly rod tip easier.

Backing and fly line is easier to practice with than is monofilament, but with a little practice, a clean, neat-looking nail knot can be completed with either material.

✦ SURGEON'S LOOP ✦

Many fly lines have a loop already installed on one end for attaching the leader. However, not all leaders have a matching loop. By using the surgeon's loop, a loop can be attached to the butt end of the leader and the two loops can be joined using the interlocking-loop method.

STEP 1:   The surgeon's loop is tied like the surgeon's knot, but with one length of line instead of two. Double the end of the line back on itself about eight inches.

STEP 2:   Holding the doubled line with your left hand, make a loop with the folded section and then pass the folded end through the loop twice.

STEP 3:   Moisten the knot and take hold of the folded end, which is now another loop, and pull tight. As a final check, place the loop over the point of a smooth tool, like your pliers or forceps, and give the knot a couple of good tugs. Trim.

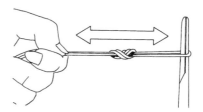

Surgeon's loop

◆ INTERLOCKING LOOPS ◆

Only when connected properly do interlocking loops make a very strong connection. If a girth hitch is used, considerable strength will be lost.

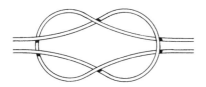

Interlocking loops

STEP 1: Let's assume that we are attaching a leader to a fly line that is on the reel. Hold the loop in the fly line in your left hand and the leader loop in your right. Pass the left loop through the right loop and squeeze both between the thumb and forefinger of your left hand.

STEP 2: Take the remaining available end on the right and pass it through the loop in the end of the fly line and pull tight. The illustration shows the proper result.

◆ NONSLIP MONO LOOP ◆

The nonslip mono loop doesn't slip and often tests close to 100 percent of the unknotted line strength. In tying this knot, the number of wraps behind the overhand knot must be precise. For lines testing 8X to six pounds, use seven turns; five turns for lines in the eight- to twelve-pound class; four turns for fifteen- to forty-pound line; three turns for fifty- or sixty-pound line; and two turns for heavier lines.

STEP 1: Put an overhand knot in the line and then pass the end through the eye of the hook. (Allow about ten inches of line the first few times.) Insert the end back through the loop in the over-hand knot, making certain it goes back through on the same side it came out originally.

STEP 2: Wrap the end around the standing leader the required number of times and insert the end back through the loop again, making sure it reenters the same side it exited.

STEP 3: Moisten the knot and start to seat it by pulling slowly on the loop or hook end. This pulls the wraps together. Before the wraps are totally tight, hold the standing part of the line in your left hand and the lure in your right hand. Pull your hands apart to finish tightening the knot, and trim.

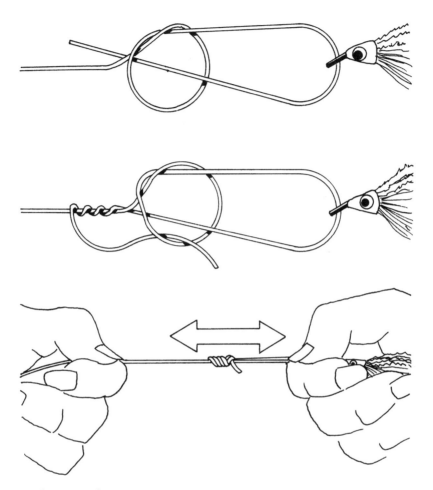

Nonslip mono loop

♦ ALBRIGHT KNOT ♦

The Albright knot is not often used in fresh water, but it is used in salt water and in situations requiring the joining of lines of greatly unequal diameters or of different materials, including mono to braided or single-strand wire.

STEP 1:   Bend a loop in the end of the heavier line and hold it with the thumb and forefinger of your left hand. Insert the end of the lighter line through the loop so the end rises above the loop about ten inches.

STEP 2:   Slip the end of the lighter line under your thumb and pinch it against the two strands of the loop. Make twelve wraps around all three strands, working from left to right. The trick lies in moving your left hand without releasing the pressure. The first

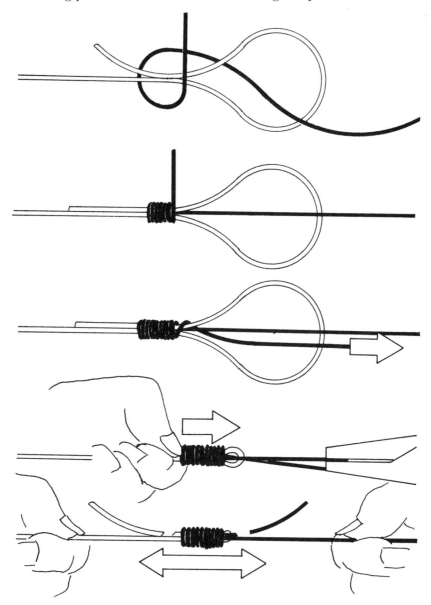

Albright knot

wrap with the tag end must reverse direction in order to move from left to right. Try to lay each wrap so that it shoulders the one before it.

STEP 3:   After completing the wraps, insert the tag end of the lighter line back through the loop so that it exits on the same side of the loop it entered. Pull gently on the standing part to jam the wraps together and start sliding them toward the closed end of the loop.

STEP 4:   Holding the heavier leader in your left hand, push the wraps with the thumb and forefinger as you pull on the light line. Work slowly so you don't slide the wraps over the end. Alternate pulling on the end of the lighter line and on the standing part until the wraps are jammed against the tag end. Use pliers to pull the tag end even tighter.

STEP 5:   Finally, pull on the standing parts of both lines to make sure the knot is secure. If you like, before trimming the light end you can lock the knot by looping the end back toward the knot and finishing it off like a Bimini twist (see page 62.)

◆ HAYWIRE TWIST ◆

The haywire twist is the strongest connection for attaching single-strand wire to a hook or for making a loop in the end of a single strand of wire.

STEP 1:   Insert the end of the wire through the eye of the hook. Then, crossing the end over the standing wire, hold the small loop in your left hand just ahead of the hook. Make sure the standing wire and the tag end cross at an angle in excess of 90 degrees.

STEP 2:   To form the haywire, you must twist both the tag end and the standing part of the wire at the same time while holding the loop securely in the other hand. This can be accomplished in half-turn increments; done correctly, each twist forms an X. Make at least three-and-a-half wraps before starting the barrel wrap.

STEP 3:   To start the barrel wrap, push the tag end until it is at right angles to the standing part. Then make several barrel wraps, making each one shoulder the wrap before it. Note that these wraps should be made one-half turn at a time. When you have made several barrel wraps, bend the tag end to form a handle that you can grasp. Rock the handle back and forth until the wire breaks.

Never cut the tag end of the wire with pliers. It leaves a burr that can slice a hand as effectively as a razor blade. When the haywire twist is completed correctly, you can run your bare hand over it and it will feel smooth.

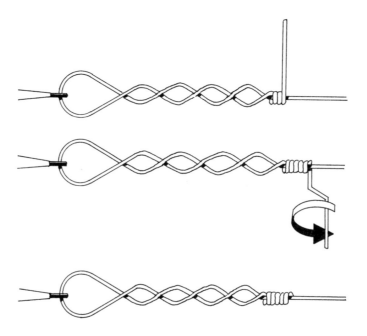

Haywire twist

♦ BIMINI TWIST ♦

The Bimini twist can be tied in monofilament or braided line to create 100 percent knot strength. The Bimini twist creates a double line with a loop in its end and forms the heart of other connection systems. Although it was developed for big-game trolling, the Bimini rates as an important knot for light tackle and fly fishing.

STEP 1: Measure about four feet of line and double the tag end back against the standing part. Grasp the standing line and the tag end between the thumb and forefinger of your left hand. Slip your right hand through the loop and push against the looped end. Rotate your right hand in a clockwise direction twenty times, putting twenty twists in the line while holding it securely in your left hand.

STEP 2: Continue to maintain pressure by holding the line securely in your left hand and pushing the back of your right hand against the closed end of the loop. Don't let the twists unwind. Bend your right knee by putting your foot on any raised object. Transfer the loop from your right hand to your knee. Keep the standing part of the line in your left hand and take the tag end in your right hand. Pull toward you with both hands simultaneously and start to separate your hands. The angle at which the standing line and tag end compress the twists should never exceed 90 degrees (45 degrees on each side of the centerline).

STEP 3: The key to this step lies in constantly maintaining a 90 degree angle between the standing line and the tag end. With the twists pushed in together (step 2), move your hands to the right at the same time. That brings the standing line directly in line with the twists and puts the tag end at a right angle to them. Pull toward you with the standing line and ease your right hand away from you slightly until the tag end jumps the first twist. As you pull on the standing line, you have to feed the tag end gradually toward the twists. Place the forefinger of your right hand against one leg of the loop and pull toward you to continue the spiral wraps.

STEP 4: Don't relax the pressure on the standing line for an instant. Slide your left hand down the standing line until you can reach the final spiral wrap with the thumb and forefinger. The loop remains over your knee. As you hold the spiral wraps between the thumb and forefinger of the left hand, use your right hand to pass the tag end around the closer leg of the loop and then back through the small loop you just created. Pull the tag end toward you until the small loop closes, and then work it back toward the spiral wraps until it locks. Now you can let go with both hands and take the main loop off your knee.

STEP 5: Hold the two legs of the loop together. About two inches to the right of the twists and spiral wraps, pass the tag end over both legs of the loop and back through the small loop created by the belly in the tag end. Do the same thing four more times, working from right to left and back toward the twists.

STEP 6: Pull the tag end toward you with your left hand as you carefully work the new spirals back toward the twist. It's a process of spreading them, pulling on the tag end, spreading, pulling, and so forth until this lock seats tightly against the Bimini twist. On lines heavier than twelve-pound test, pull the tag end with a pair of pliers after hand-tightening to add a final tightening.

STEP 7:   Trim the tag end close to the knot.

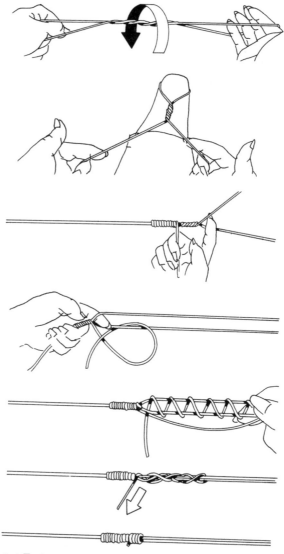

Bimini Twist

◆ ARBOR KNOT ◆

This arbor knot is easy to tie and does the job well. It's strong enough to hold if a rod and reel go overboard and you have to pull them up with the line.

STEP 1:   Circle the arbor of the spool with the tag end of the line. Then tie an overhand knot around the standing line.

STEP 2:   Tie a second overhand knot in the tag end no more than two or three inches from the first overhand knot.

STEP 3:   Moisten the line and the two overhand knots. Hold the reel or spool in your left hand and pull on the standing part of the line with your right hand. The first overhand knot will slide down to the arbor and the second overhand knot will serve as a jam. Trim the tag end so that it doesn't catch line stored on the spool.

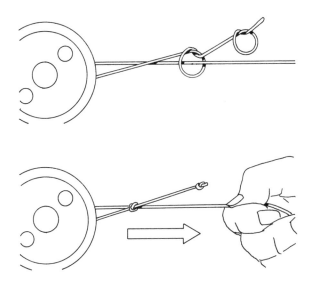

Arbor knot

◆ QUICK-RELEASE KNOT ◆

This is a handy knot that can be used for all sorts of things, like tying a tarp to a tree, or a canoe to a dock, or a dog to a post, and so on.

STEP 1:   Pass the tag end of the line around a post or other object and under the standing line. Allow a tag end of about two feet to complete the knot.

STEP 2:   Reach through the loop created in step 1 and pull the tag line through partially, forming a second loop. Be sure that the very end of the tag line does not get pulled through.

STEP 3:   Pull gently on the standing line to close the main loop partially.

STEP 4:   Reach through the second loop created in step 2 and grip the tag end in its center, pulling it partially through the loop.

STEP 5:   Pull the standing part of the line to tighten the quick-release and the knot will hold. Tug on the tag end and the knot comes apart instantly.

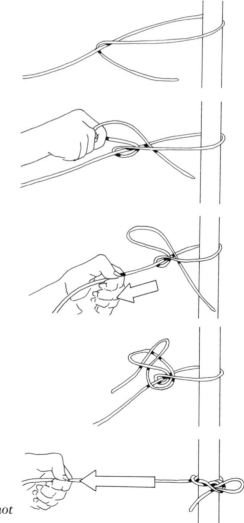

Quick-release knot

◆ NONSLIP SHOELACE KNOT ◆

Aboard a boat or in the field, this method for tying your shoes will keep the laces from loosening. If you have children, you may want to teach it to them.

STEP 1: Cross one lace over the other and snug it up just as if you were tying your shoes the standard way.

STEP 2: Double back a tag end to form one loop of a bow and pass the other end in front of this loop.

STEP 3: Continue passing the tag end around the loop and behind it. Take another complete turn with the tag end around the loop. Then bend the lace near the tag end to double it and push the doubled end through the center of the two turns, forming the other side of the bow.

STEP 4: Tighten the bow by pulling on both loops. With some laces, you may have to tease them a little bit to make the bow uniform. The finished knot will not loosen by itself.

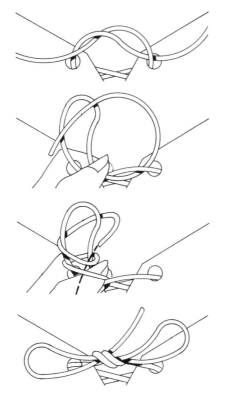

Nonslip shoelace knot

5

CASTING: THE HEART OF THE SPORT

BARRY AND I STARTED DATING IN THE FALL of 1979. I remember standing in the snow in his driveway that first winter as he taught me to cast a fly rod. I had no idea what fly fishing was, but I knew I wanted to spend time with this guy and it sounded like once spring came he was going to spend every spare minute on the trout stream.

I was fortunate: Barry was a fly-fishing instructor. At the time I didn't realize the importance of good instruction, but I do now. I've been teaching people how to fly fish for over ten years, and one thought comes to my mind over and over again: If you have any choice, don't try to teach yourself to cast, and don't try to learn from someone you love. It worked for me then because we were young, in love, and anxious to please each other—I'm not so sure it would work today. It's very rare indeed that an individual can teach someone she loves anything, and this goes for husbands, wives, sons, or daughters.

There are many excellent instructors and fly-fishing school. There's nothing like hands-on instruction from an experienced teacher. Good instruction will save you time and get you quickly to where you can confidently go out on your own.

As we begin to grasp the mechanics of fly casting, we'll all be a little bit different from one another. We will each develop our own casting style, our own identity. Thank goodness! What a boring world this would be if we all held our pencils, signed our names, ate spaghetti, tied flies, and fished the same way. We'd be clones. So get some good help and then step out on your own and experiment!

After instruction, or in addition to it, a book can be a great reference for troubleshooting and advancing. But I have to admit that learning to cast from a book—any book—is not easy. It's difficult to put into writing what I can easily demonstrate while you are standing beside me.

I was a freshwater-only fisherman for many years. When I started fishing in salt water, I suddenly realized my casting was totally inadequate. Barry was okay in most situations because of his strength—he's six foot one with strong arms. I'm five foot four without strong arms. With the casting style we were using, I ended up sitting in the boat watching a lot of the time. I was using a lot of wrist in my casting and it's hard not to use the wrist when you've grown used to it. I had to learn that the rod makes the cast with the help of my arm—not the other way around.

After a couple of frustrating years, I contacted Lefty Kreh and sought help. Lefty, in the years to follow, would redefine fly casting for me. It's been hard to forget everything and learn all over again. Lefty's style is definitely different from the traditional casting methods that have been handed down through the years. His style is what I now use in fresh and salt water. I guarantee that if you use this method, you'll be a much better caster and will be able to handle fishing situations most women could only dream about a few years ago.

Fly fishing is a sport full of wonderful, exciting experiences—don't let frustration with learning to cast ruin it for you. Fly casting doesn't require a lot of muscle or power. (Of course, any that you have will help!) It does take understanding, patience, and determination. In just a short time, you'll see that casting is rewarding and fun. After all, you can be in the right place with the right fly, but if you can't present it properly to the fish, you might as well go home. Casting is the heart of the sport.

GETTING READY

A graphite fly rod from eight feet to nine feet in length, rated for a 5- or 6-weight line with an attached nine-foot 4X tapered leader is an excellent first outfit. The line should be a weight-forward floating line and should be installed on a trout reel with backing. The backing is not necessary for casting, but it is for fishing, and this outfit will also be a favorite for trout and panfish. It is important to have the reel fastened on the rod correctly. Make sure the line is coming off the bottom of the reel and that you crank forward to bring the line back on the reel.

It's important to find a good place to practice your casting. I hope you can find a lawn, park, golf course, or ballfield near your home. A pond or lake with a mowed edge is excellent—if you

An illustration of proper grip.

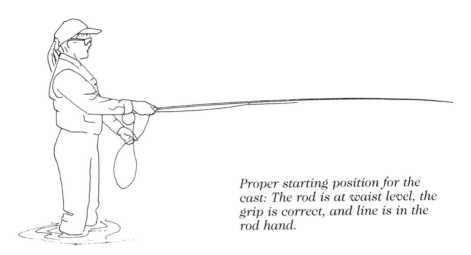

Proper starting position for the cast: The rod is at waist level, the grip is correct, and line is in the rod hand.

won't be distracted by the fish. You must be able to concentrate on casting, not on fishing, so usually plain grass is best. This place should be fairly quiet without noisy children running around (especially if they're your own). A practice session should be about twenty minutes. More than that and you'll get tired and start making mistakes. Two or three sessions a week is perfect.

When you get to this place, put the rod together, run the line through the guides, and pull the leader through the tip-top. Pick up the rod and pull what seems to be twenty-five feet of line off the reel, letting it coil in front of you on the grass. Lay the rod down beside the coils and, holding the leader, walk the line out so it lies straight out in front of the rod tip on the grass. Use a tape measure or a yardstick to measure the line, and with a black permanent marker, mark the line at twenty-five feet. A small mark is fine. Reel in any extra so the mark is at the end of the rod tip. When you practice next time, you won't have to guess or measure again. (This twenty-five feet does not include the leader. With a nine-foot leader, you'll be casting thirty-four feet, which is an ideal length to start with.)

Pick up the rod in your prominent hand (right for most of us), using the grip shown in the illustration on the opposite page, with thumb on top. You might want to experiment with your index finger on top, but there is more muscle, therefore more power, in your thumb. For that reason, the preferred grip is with the thumb on top. Having your thumb on top will also help control and dis-

Here is the wrong way to begin the cast, with the rod tip pointed up. Unfortunately, this is where most people think they should start.

cipline the rod, and most of us find this the most comfortable grip. Hold the fly line against the cork handle inside your "rod hand." Later we will move it to the other hand, which will become the "line hand," but for now it should stay in the rod hand.

Keep the rod tip pointed forward, parallel toward the ground, and at waist level. The rod tip should never be pointed upward, yet, oddly enough, that's where it's usually pointed! When the rod tip is lifted above parallel, it becomes more difficult to start the cast because of the extra line between the rod tip and the grass. Practice holding the rod without letting the tip lift.

If you're right-handed, your left foot should be slightly ahead of your right. This will allow your body to rock back and forth slightly with the cast, balancing your weight.

There should not be a fly on the end of the leader. Getting comfortable with controlling the line and knowing where it is at all times will make it easier later to cast flies. If you like, you can tie a bit of orange yarn on the end of the leader. The yarn will help you see where the fly would actually land, if it were attached. Be careful that you don't use too much—the yarn can be wind-resistent and difficult to cast. You want just enough to see on the grass.

You are now in your starting position.

Here is a side view of the progression of the backcast. Notice that the rod never drops below waist level.

THE BACKCAST

The backcast starts with the rod in front and sweeps to the stopping position behind us. The backcast is the setup for the forward cast, and it must be good in order for the forward cast to be good.

In our starting position, the thumb is on top of the rod handle. The hand and wrist should be turned outward about 45 degrees from the body. You should be able to see your fingernails and the palm of your hand—not flat, as you would if you were going to show someone a bug trapped in your hand, but at a tilt so that the rod is away from your body but still pointed upward. This outward position allows your arm to

Poor arm positioning for the backcast.

Here is a view of the 180-degree plane of the backcast.

move through a longer arc than it would by staying close. It also keeps the fly and fly line away from you during casting.

The cast is made using the forearm. It's critical that the wrist remain straight—don't let it hinge or break at the end of the cast. This is a very common mistake because you can get away with it on short casts. But later on, when you need to make a nice long cast, you'll have developed a terrible habit that's almost impossible to correct. Watch your wrist as you cast and make sure it's behaving.

The elbow should never be above the shoulder. There is no need to reach up with the rod. Your arm may often be extended out in front of your shoulder or behind it, but it should never be higher than your shoulder. This is another easy mistake that will result in stressed, tired shoulders and a backache.

The elbow and the upper arm will move back and forth with the forearm, but the forearm does the work. The upper arm will supply muscle power to the forearm with the elbow acting like a pivot point from which the forearm moves. Keep the elbow down at your side where it's comfortable but not rigid. There should be space between your ribs and elbow.

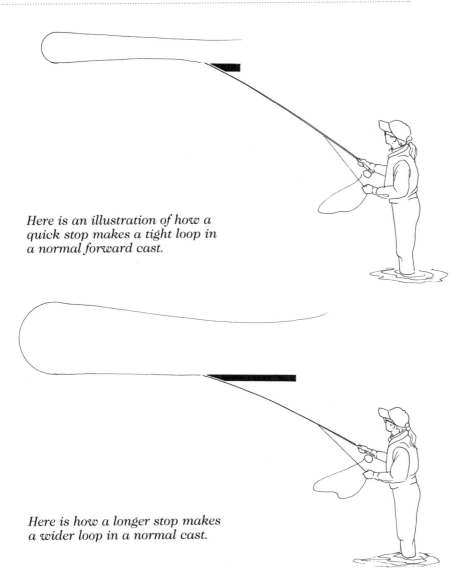

Here is an illustration of how a quick stop makes a tight loop in a normal forward cast.

Here is how a longer stop makes a wider loop in a normal cast.

We are now ready to cast. Look behind you to make sure you have plenty of room for the backcast. Then look ahead about thirty feet and pick an imaginery target and face it squarely, with your feet in the proper position. Placing a hat or a paper plate on the grass will give you a visible target. Later on, use several for target practice. The rod tip during the backcast has to be in line with the target. The backcast, if it straightened out behind us on the grass, would be 180 degrees from the target. This is what we mean when we say "keep the cast in plane." If one end or the other kicks out of plane, the cast will not be accurate. You can move the rod tip out of plane to change the direction of the cast, but only *after* you complete the cast. A reach cast, explained later on, is a good example of this.

The cast itself is a slow, progressive sweep speeding up to a real quick, short stop. If you start too fast, you'll rip the line off the grass. When you're fishing, this kind of action will scare the fish. Start the cast by slowly pulling the rod back, and as soon as you see the end of the fly line start to move (in most casts this is about the time your rod is passing by your head), speed up quickly, lifting the rest of the line into the air, and bring the rod tip to a quick, sharp stop in the back. Once you start a cast, don't change your mind for anything short of an emergency. You'll only pull the line back on top of you, and it will be difficult to get started again.

There is no magic stopping point in the back. Where the rod stops will change as the amount of line that you're casting varies. Make sure the rod tip is always well behind your shoulder and pointing up. The rod tip should always be above parallel to the ground at the end of the backcast. If the rod tip goes too far back or dips down, you'll lose power, the cast will open up, and the line will sag. It's then hard to keep it from hitting the grass—and the water when you're fishing. This will cause your forward cast to look bogged down and sloppy (because it is). This will also happen if there is no quick speed-up and stop at the end of the cast.

Remember, you should feel the quick, short stop in the rod tip as you complete the cast. If the rod stops too short, it gets in the way of the line coming back and the two will often collide. Turn around and watch the cast: every time it stops at the correct position, a nice loop results. With practice, you'll develop a habit, and soon your arm will be stopping without being watched. Check your wrist here, too. The thumb should be in line with your forearm, not perpendicular to it.

A short acceleration (speed-up) at the end combined with a quick stop will give you a narrow loop. Narrow (or tight) loops are preferred for most casts. A wide loop is made by a longer acceleration and a slower stop. This is true at either end of the cast. This acceleration and quick stop are critical to a good cast. The rod speeds up at the end and then stops dead in its tracks.

It's a combination of this speed-up and dead stop (without any wrist action) that programs the loop. You'll want a narrow loop when fishing weightless dry flies. But when you're fishing weighted nymphs, streamers, or saltwater flies, you'll want a wider loop. It's important that you understand and know how to tighten and widen (or open up) the loop. This is one of the most important casting exercises you can practice.

THE FORWARD CAST

As soon as the backcast is stopped, the forward cast should begin. As you become more experienced, you'll understand that how long the "stop" is depends on how much line you're casting. The stop is necessary to allow most of the line time to pass by the rod tip before you start to move it in the opposite direction. The longer the cast, the longer the stop. It's all timing, and that comes from experience. For the time being, with the amount of line you're casting, as soon as you stop completely, you can start forward again.

At the end of the backcast, your arm should be behind and slightly below your shoulder, with the palm of your hand and your fingernails facing you. Your thumb should be pointed up. The forward cast is just a little different. The arm has basically the same job coming forward as it does going back.

A side view of the progression of a forward cast.

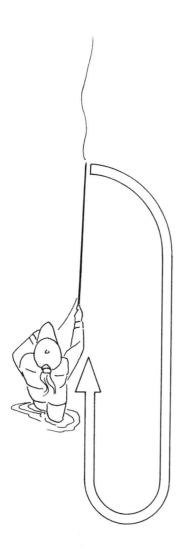

An overhead view of an oval cast.

As you start to move your arm forward through the casting arc, your wrist should roll or rotate smoothly counterclockwise through the end of the cast. This slight roll allows the line coming forward to avoid the line that may still be going back. This will be especially important on long casts. If you start this habit in the beginning, you'll be comfortable with it when the time comes for long casts. It will also help the line avoid hitting the rod. This wrist rotation results in a slightly oval cast.

The arm continues through the cast and into the speed-up and stop, the acceleration and quick stop at the front end. At the end of the cast, the rod and the thumb are directly in line with the target at about eye level. "In line" is simply that—it does not mean pointed at as in aiming with a gun.

If the rod tip is not brought forward enough, slack line falls off the end of the rod (because it's too high) and the cast will be shorter than expected. In addition, because the rod tip stopped too high, the leader can collide with the line, causing a tailing loop (the line dips and hits the leader on the way through) and can result in a tangle.

If you find that you're still hitting the line with the leader during the cast, here's the solution: At the very end of the cast, after the speed-up and stop, simply drop the rod tip a couple of inches. This will pull the lower part of the loop just a little lower and out of the way of the top part. If you drop it too much, you'll pull the loop apart and lose line speed and control. Just two inches is all you need. Not everyone has this problem; there's no need to try to correct it if you don't have it.

An occasional problem is too much power. This problem will show up more often with men than women, but it can happen to women, too. We know that it's important for the rod to come to a complete stop at each end of the cast. If there is too much power in the cast, it shocks the rod, which in turn sends shock waves out through the line. The line then jumps around and does not look smooth. If you see the rod tip stop, then dance around a bit, you're probably giving it too much power, thus shocking the cast. The rod tip is oscillating. Lighten up, use a little less power, and come smoothly and quickly to a dead stop before starting in the opposite direction.

To present the fly to the water, after the rod stops out front at eye level, let the line start to straighten. Then, lower the rod tip with the line as it falls to the water. If you don't bring the rod tip down with the line, you'll end up with a shorter cast than expected and the rod will be pointing up—where you don't want it. On the other hand, if you bring the rod tip down too quickly, you'll drive the cast hard into the water and the leader will crash in a tangled mess. By stopping or slowing the rod tip enough to allow the cast to unroll above the water, a couple of things happen: You allow the energy to leave the cast so the line and leader land delicately and noiselessly on the water. And you can judge the distance, if you're fishing, to a particular target. By watching your fly in midair, you can determine whether you have too much line out, not enough, or just the right amount to reach the fish.

As the amount of line you're casting increases, the stroke (or path of the rod) should lengthen. In other words, you'll want to move your arm farther back behind you and farther out in front on the forward cast. For shorter distances, like our twenty-five feet, we don't have to move the rod as far back as we would for forty feet. The more line you have to move, the longer the distance should be that you have to move it through. And as the line increases, so must the power from your arm. But don't confuse power with speed. Moving your arm fast without power will cause the undisciplined line to fall, wrapping around you and tangling.

FALSE CASTS

A "false" cast doesn't go anywhere except back and forth. We false cast when we practice our casting and when we are trying out a new rod. By false casting we can get a feel for how the rod will perform. We also false cast when we're fishing. It helps dry our dry flies by shaking out the water as the fly travels through the air. It buys us some time if we're studying a particular fish or a spot where we think we might have seen a fish. By false casting a couple of times, we can delay making a commitment until we're sure of the target. Sometimes we'll use it when we're changing directions with our cast. But most important, false casting helps us increase line speed. (Line speed is how fast the line moves back and forth and will be discussed later.)

We false cast on the grass as well as on the water. The line is kept in the air and does not hit the grass (or water) until we're ready to complete the cast. False casting is a very important practice exercise because it helps us develop timing and rhythm.

When practicing, make five or six false casts and then complete the cast, allowing the line to lie extended on the grass. Pick up the line and make five or six casts again. Casting too many times without resting will tire your arm, so don't overdo it!

ROD LOADING

"Loading the rod" refers to how much or how little the combination of rod action and line weight bends or flexes the rod during the cast. Each rod responds differently, and it's a proper mix of the two that puts the spring into the cast, or loads the rod.

Blisters most commonly occur from grasping the rod too tightly. I've never seen a rod fly out of anyone's hand! So try to loosen your grip as you move the rod from one end of the cast to the other. You need more grip strength during the speed-up and stop at each end than you do through the middle. After about five minutes of casting, put the rod in the other hand and shake out your rod hand, flex your fingers, and rest for a minute before starting up again. As you become comfortable with your casting and equipment, you should find that you're not gripping the rod as hard as you were in the beginning.

SHOOTING LINE & RETRIEVING

After a couple of practice sessions, you'll be comfortable with the backcast, forward cast, and presentation (completing the cast). Now you're ready to shoot line, which simply means allowing additional line to slide out through the guides at the end of the forward cast.

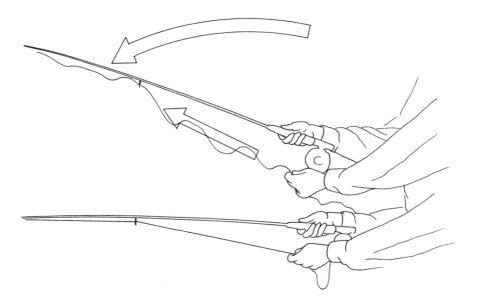

Shooting line: bottom Keep the line hand and the rod hand as well synchronized as possible throughout the cast; top allow the line to slide forward out of the line hand at the end of the forward cast.

Move the line over to your other hand. You now have a rod hand and a line hand. The line should always be in one hand or the other. Never let it hang unattended in the water—a fish can hit the fly at any time! If you don't have control of the line, you won't be able to catch the fish.

Using the same starting position, pull line off the reel until you have several coils laying on the grass in front of you. There should not be any slack between the stripping guide and your line hand; the extra line should be on the grass between your hand and the reel.

Start to cast as you always do, but let the line hand follow the rod hand as much or as little as is comfortable. It's good if you can keep the two hands about eight inches apart throughout the cast. By keeping the hands in sync with each other, no slack line will accumulate between them.

Once you're comfortable with the timing and rhythm (after four or five false casts), at the very end of the forward cast, when the rod is pointed ahead during the speed-up and stop, let the line slide out of your line hand. While the line is sliding out of your line hand, your rod hand should be lowering the rod tip as the cast is completed. During the false casts, you will need to build line speed (moving the rod faster through the cast) while still remembering your speed-up and stop at each end. Don't concentrate so hard on the release of line that you forget the quick stop at the end of the last forward cast. If you don't have the line speed and the quick stop at the end, there won't be enough energy to pick up and carry the extra line that you're shooting.

It's easy to let the fly line slide out of your line hand too soon. You can't let go of the line before the quick stop at the end of the cast. If you do, it won't go anywhere. Wait until you've completed the speed-up and stop and the rod is pointing ahead.

As you're slowly lowering the rod tip, the line will be sliding through the guides. Don't let it slip out of your line hand. With a little practice, the line will easily slide through your hand with your thumb and fingertips touching to form an O-ring. If you keep your hand closed loosely around the line, it won't get tangled around the reel on the way out, and you can quickly get it back (if you've misjudged distance) by simply closing your hand and tugging it back. Once more, you're staying in control of the line.

If the line doesn't shoot out, it's probably for one of these reasons:

1.   You're forgetting line speed and the speed-up and stop at each end of the cast.

2.   You're letting the line slide out of your hand too soon (probably) or too late (unlikely).

3.   Your line may need to be cleaned (see chapter 4).

4.   Check to make sure the fly line is not wrapped around the rod somewhere and that you haven't missed a guide.

5.   Make sure you're not holding the line with both hands.

Shooting line is fun. Almost everyone is surprised when it happens the first time. We shoot line often when we're fishing. For example: We're standing midstream with thiry feet of clearance behind us, but the fish we want to catch is thirty-five feet in front of us. If we try to cast thirty-five feet, we'll obviously get the line caught in the trees behind us. So we cast thirty feet and shoot five to reach the fish.

Shooting line is also helpful when we need to make long casts. As long as the cast has good line speed and energy (the speed-up and stop at the end), we can shoot line. On long casts, keep the rod tip a little higher so the cast doesn't crash before it unrolls. We can shoot a little line on each false cast or a lot of line on the last cast. If too much line is shot, there won't be enough

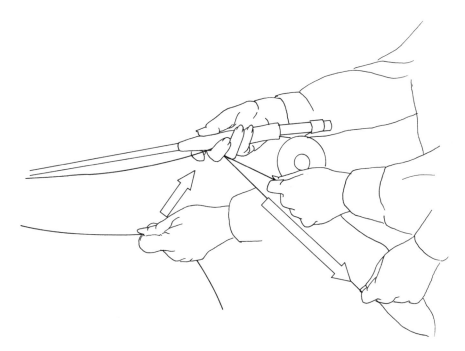

Retrieving line: Make sure the line is held in the rod hand and pulled back and down by the line hand through the rod hand.

energy to turn the cast over, and the line and leader will collapse on the water. Experience and practice are the best teachers of knowing how much line we can handle. The more experienced we become, the more line we can shoot.

Now that the line is out there, we need to get it back. Eventually, you'll be able to pick up a lot of line and start to cast again, but for now, let's practice retrieving.

As soon as the line is on the grass, hand the line back to your rod hand. You can easily slip it under the middle or ring finger of the rod hand. This will free up your line hand to do other jobs: get things out of your vest, adjust your sunglasses, brush your hair out of your eyes, and do the retrieving.

Retrieving means bringing in the line a little at a time. Once the line is hooked under a finger of the rod hand, reach up with your line hand and pull about fourteen inches of line through the other hand. Let go, reach up, and do it again. This is retrieving. Make sure you're reaching up behind (not in front of) the rod hand and pulling the line through the hand.

When retrieving the line to cast again, we want long, quick

strips, or retrieves, getting the line back as quickly as possible. But when we're retrieving to swim flies through the water, we sometimes want short slow retrieves, or short fast retrieves; in salt water, we often want long fast retrieves. It depends on why and what we're retrieving. Always stay alert and ready for a strike, and don't be afraid to experiment!

Be careful that you don't retrieve too much line. Keep an eye on the end of the fly line, and start to cast when at least ten feet of fly line is still beyond the rod tip. It's hard, especially in the beginning, to start casting again with less than ten feet of fly line.

At this point, you've mastered basic casting. When you go out to practice, you should be able to do the following:

1.   Easily pick up and lay down the initial twenty-five feet of line with the leader turning over and the yarn gently landing at the end of the cast.

2.   Complete step 1, incorporating a couple of false casts.

3.   While false casting, change direction. Move the rod forward in a new direction while the line is back behind you at the end of the backcast. Don't forget your targets. Start with them about fifteen feet apart and move them to new positions as you practice.

4.   Shoot line, retrieve it back, and shoot again while keeping the rod tip low during the retrieve and the line under control in your hand at all times.

5.   Cast narrow or wide loops by increasing or decreasing the line speed and the speed-up and stop.

6.   Make smooth, neat casts without the leader hitting the rod.

CASTS FOR SPECIAL SITUATIONS

ROLL CAST

This cast is used in a number of situations but most commonly whenever it's windy or when there is no room for a backcast. A roll cast is also useful when fishing weighted nymphs or streamers, because it eliminates the need to false cast. Therefore, flies

Beginning a roll cast by slowly bringing the rod toward the shoulder, allowing the line to slide across the water.

Continuing the roll cast by stopping the rod tip briefly so the line comes to a stop.

Making the forward roll cast, keeping the rod in a sidearm position, away from the body.

stay wet and sink quickly. A roll ca is pretty much a forward cast starting from a high starting position.

To complete a roll cast, slowly bring the rod back behind your shoulder, allowing the line to slide across the water toward you. Stop the rod tip for just a second so the line that is following the rod can come almost to a stop. The longer the cast, the farther back you'll have to bring the rod tip. Make the forward cast, keeping the rod in a sidearm position, away from your body. The sidearm position will help prevent the slack line from tangling around the rod, and it keeps the fly away from you on windy days. Don't forget to speed-up and stop on the forward cast in the direction you want the fly to go. At the end of the cast, the rod should be at about eye level. Don't allow the rod tip to dip low in the front. If this happens, the cast won't have time to unroll before collapsing on the water.

SIDEARM CAST

This cast is no different from our initial cast except that it's more parallel to the water. It is used for getting under over-hanging limbs and branches on either the forward cast or the backcast, and for casting on windy days. Try to keep the rod tip on the same plane during the cast. The distance between the rod and the water should be the same each end of the cast. This is a helpful cast and a good one to practice on the lawn.

Contrast the high rod position of this normal cast with the proper sidearm-cast rod position.

The proper rod position in a sidearm cast.

REACH CAST

This and the sidearm cast are my two most-often-used casts. The reach cast is sometimes called "aerial mending." The result is the same on both the reach and the mend casts.

To understand a reach cast, we need to have a clear picture of stream current. Let's say the stream is flowing from left to right; therefore, downstream is to the right. We are casting across fast water to a fish on the "seam," where the fast and slow water meet. Because the water in front of us is moving faster than the water

Here is an overhead view of the reach cast: After the speed-up-and-stop, move the rod to the left.

the fish is in, the fly will drag almost immediately if we use a conventional cast.

False cast as you would ordinarily, but on the last cast, as the line is unrolling, reach up and across to the left after the speed-up and stop. For right-handed people, your right hand should move through a half-moon arc, ending up in front of your left shoulder with your right elbow near eye level. As soon as the line is on the water, drop the rod tip and move it back to the right to lead the cast. Because you completed the speed-up and stop first, the fly will go to the fish. The reach will position the line and leader upstream of the fly, we hope allowing the fly to sit for a couple of seconds while the current carries the leader and line down to the fly. When they catch up, the fly will be dragged out and the cast will be done. With luck, the fish will take the fly while it sits there.

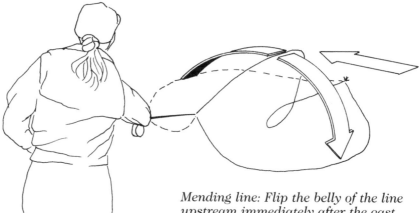

Mending line: Flip the belly of the line upstream immediately after the cast has been completed.

MENDING LINE

Mending line is done as soon as the cast is on the water. We almost always mend the line upstream. So, using the above situation, if we want to mend instead of reach, we would make an ordinary cast to the fish. As soon as the line is on the water, using the rod tip, lift some of the line up and flip it upstream. Hold a little extra line loosely in your line hand: Once you lift the rod tip and flip, use the slack line in the flip. By using the slack line, you'll have to pick less up and there will be more line on the water as a result. It's important to *lift* and flip the line upstream and not drag it up across the surface. Dragging the line upstream will form a "belly" of line and put tension on the fly. The line should be lifted off the water and flipped upstream immediately after the cast is completed. If you wait more than a second or two, the available slack in the cast will be used up and the mend won't be possible.

Mending is often used with streamer fishing because the extra slack allows the fly to sink faster and deeper. If the water is fast, we can mend several times before retrieving.

Mending with dry flies requires some fine-tuning. If we lift the rod tip too high or flip too hard, we'll move the fly immediately, causing drag and defeating our purpose. For this reason, a reach cast is often easier with dry flies.

FLUTTERING CAST

This technique is also very helpful and easy to learn. It creates additional slack in the cast for a longer drag-free drift on dry flies. As with the other casts, it starts with an ordinary cast. During the final presentation cast, stop the rod tip just a little higher than usual, and as the line is unrolling, flutter the rod tip up and down a couple of inches once or twice. This will pull the leader back just

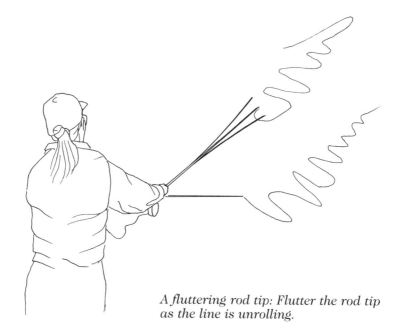

A fluttering rod tip: Flutter the rod tip as the line is unrolling.

a few inches, causing slack to form in the air before the line and leader land on the water. This fluttering action will give you a few extra coils of line on the water without sacrificing a smooth turnover of the leader and fly.

DOUBLE HAULING

Double hauling quickly increases line speed, making long casts possible with just two or three false casts. Again, it starts out with a basic cast with extra line pulled off the reel and lying in coils in front of you, with the line in your line hand. The rod hand does the normal casting routine with the line hand following six to ten inches away on the backcast and leading the same distance on the forward cast.

The line hand performs the haul or tug at the same time the rod hand is doing the speed-up and stop. The hauls should be very short (four inches) and very fast, one at the end of the backcast and one at the end of the forward cast. The haul increases the line speed, enabling the caster to shoot an impressive amount of line.

Double hauling *sounds* easy. In practice, it is very much like patting your head and rubbing your stomach at the same time. It's not as easy as it looks. It's not difficult, but it will take some patience and determination to master. If you find you're all thumbs, let the cast straighten out on the grass at the end of the backcast. Think about what you need to do before starting into the forward cast. Repeat this procedure at the end of the forward cast as well.

Once you get it, you'll wonder what was so hard. Double hauling is useful whenever long casts are required and on windy days, when a faster line will cut through the wind better than a slower line will.

There are many casts to learn, and sometimes the same casts have a couple of different names. I've described my most useful casts, using their most common names. As you become more experienced, there will be other casts for you to add to your fishing repertoire. As with everything, practice makes perfect!

Beginning the double haul: The line hand should follow the rod hand on the back-cast by six to ten inches.

Continuing the double haul: At the end of the backcast, tug with the line hand—make it short and fast.

Continuing the double haul: Bringing the rod forward after the back-cast "haul."

Continuing the double haul: Another short and fast tug is made with the line hand at the end of the forward cast.

WOOLLY BUGGERS DON'T HATCH: FRESHWATER FLY SELECTION

FLIES ARE THE ARTIFICIAL DECEIVERS THAT we attach to the end of our tapered leader. How important are they? They can be the difference between success and failure. It's amazing how little importance is sometimes given to fly selection or fly quality. We can spend a lot of money on a fine fly rod and reel, but in the end it's the fly that the fish accepts or refuses. We cannot become good fly fishermen without some knowledge of flies.

Flies are not made by a machine—never were, probably never will be. They are tied by hand by a person, a fly tier. Starting with a hook, the fly tier will use carefully selected

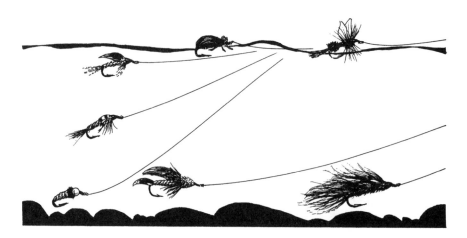

Flies on and in the water. Dry flies float, nymphs sink to varying degrees, and streamers move underneath.

natural or synthetic materials and thread, and with a few specialized tools will create a fly that looks like something the fish want to eat.

Flies that *imitate* are tied to look like a minnow, a crustacean, a particular insect, or a stage of an insect that a fish would eat. Flies that *attract* are tied to do just that, attract the fish. These are sometimes colorful flies, and through color, motion, and size produce a response from the fish.

Don't panic when you look into a friend's vest and find boxes filled with literally hundreds of flies. You can start with a small but focused selection of fly patterns, have fun, and catch fish. But as you become more experienced, you'll find yourself adding a few flies here and there, and soon you, too, will have boxes full!

All flies, whether they attract or imitate, fall into two basic fly groups: *dry* flies and *wet* flies. Dry flies are those that float on the surface of the water. Because they float, you can usually see them. Wet flies sink and are fished under the surface. Within these two basic groups are subgroups. In other words, dry flies include standard dry flies, spinners, floating terrestrials, and other floating flies. Wet flies include nymphs, emergers, streamers, and sinking terrestrials. If a fisherman says he is fishing "drys," he means the flies float. If he says he is fishing "wets," he is fishing flies that sink under the water.

Nymphs imitate an underwater stage of an aquatic insect. *Emergers* imitate an advanced form of an aquatic insect that is

My seven favorite freshwater flies: 1. Henryville Caddis, 2. Royal Wulff, 3. Adams, 4. Clouser Minnow, 5. Woolly Bugger, 6. Hare's Ear Nymph, 7. Pleasant-Tail Nymph.

swimming toward the water surface to hatch into an adult. *Streamers* imitate baitfish (small fish that large fish feed on), or leeches, sculpins, and so on. Often, they are simply a lure-type fly that coaxes a reaction from a fish because of color and motion. They look alive.

Names for flies are generally arrived at by the fly tier or fisherman who first came up with the idea for the pattern, or the name may simply imply what the fly imitates. For instance, the Goddard Caddis is a caddis pattern developed by a British fly tier named John Goddard. On the other hand, the Hare's Ear Nymph is a simple nymph tied with the fur from a hare's (rabbit) ear or mask. An Early Black Stonefly Nymph is a pattern for the early-season black stonefly nymph.

We have several popular attractor dry flies that catch trout and panfish. My favorite is the Adams. Although the Adams does not imitate any specific insect, its blend of gray and brown colors make it buggy looking. I carry it in five sizes: 12, 14, 16, 18, and 20. One of these sizes will match the size of most any insect I see on the water. There are a few fishermen who use *only* this fly.

My next favorite is a true attractor: the Royal Wulff. With a red-floss body band and white calf-hair wings, it clearly resembles no insect I have ever seen. Yet it floats high and is very visible, especially in fast water. RW's (a nickname from long ago) work well on wild brook trout and even bluegills. At the right time of year, it's possible to have a thirty-fish day twitching a Royal Wulff alongside lily pads or through the runs of a favorite brook trout stream. I carry RW's in sizes 12 and 14.

My third choice is a Henryville Caddis. Although the name indicates an insect category, the Henryville is not tied to imitate a particular caddisfly. Like the Adams, I carry the Henryville in sizes 12 through 20. With these three dry flies, I can confidently fish on the surface and expect to catch fish.

A Gold-Ribbed Hare's Ear Nymph is hard to beat for fishing under water. It's a popular pattern and easily found in most fly shops. I carry it in sizes 10, 14, and 18. A Pheasant Tail Nymph in sizes 16 and 20 works well when a smaller nymph pattern is needed. These are effective nymph patterns, and most of the time one or the other will be close enough to match a nymph that the fish will recognize.

To round out our underwater selection, there are two streamer patterns that I always carry. The first is a black Woolly Bugger. This is a strange name for a fly that has taken most fresh- and many saltwater species of fish. It's a wonderful *search* pattern, and I carry Woolly Buggers in size 6 for larger trout and bass and in sizes 8 and 10 for general trout fishing. A smaller size 12 works well for panfish. If I could carry only one streamer, it would be a Woolly Bugger.

If I could only carry two streamers, the second would be a Clouser Deep Minnow. This streamer has lead eyes that help it sink deep and fast. Bob Clouser, the fly's inventor, ties it in a variety of colors. I like his fox squirrel version best. I carry Clouser Minnows in size 6 for smallmouth bass and 8 and 10 for general trout fishing.

The above seven flies in the recommended sizes will give you a good start. They are all popular patterns and should be easy to find in fly shops and catalogs.

A good source of regional information is your local fly shop. When I'm traveling and fishing, I always check with the local shop. One of the most commonly asked questions in any fly shop is "What flies are working?" You'll usually find the answers there, with helpful information and suggestions. You may hear names like Quill Gordon, Hendrickson, or Light Cahill. There may be talk of caddis or stoneflies. It may be terrestrial season with suggestions of ants, grasshoppers, or beetles. Or, to confuse you even more, it might be mentioned that male Paraleptophlebia spinners are falling about four in the afternoon, so make sure you have some. At this point, you may just want to throw in the towel and head home.

Don't be intimidated. Actually it's not as complicated as it sounds. Listen to the advice, and ask the clerk to show you the flies. All insects have common and Latin names. Thank goodness most fly fishermen use the common names. If the clerk suggests a certain fly, always buy a couple. You'll be better prepared, having an extra should you lose one on a fish or in a tree. There's nothing more frustrating than to lose the one and only fly the fish will take.

Trout can become extremely selective. As well-rounded fly fishermen, we should learn as much as we can about the habits and food sources of the fish. Most of a trout's diet consists of insects, mostly aquatic, but often landborn (terrestrial).

We're all a little overwhelmed when we first hear all the insect jargon. But most of the insects found on trout streams are harmless. Of course, there are exceptions like bees and mosquitoes. Most are vital to the environment, they feed fish and birds, and often hang in a very delicate balance with nature. A lot of anglers take great pleasure in keeping a journal that lists and describes all insects found on a particular day. The habit of keeping a journal will make you more observant.

Frankly, the trout doesn't care if the insect it is eating is a Tricorythodes or a Trico (the common name). There is a time and place for proper Latin names, but it is not necessary in a basic introduction to insects on which trout feed.

MAYFLIES

The mayfly is a major food source for fish. There are hundreds of different mayflies, but perhaps only eighteen to twenty that we, as fly fishermen, need to recognize. The good news is that they hatch on a calendar schedule and, as the chart on page 97 shows us, have common names. They look the same every year in size and color, which makes them easy to remember.

There are four stages in the mayfly life cycle that are important to the fly fisherman: nymph, emerger, dun, and spinner. Generally, the mayfly lives for about a year, and most of that time is spent under water, in the *nymph* stage. The mayfly nymphs

The life cycle of the mayfly.

cling to rocks or burrow in the silty bottom of the stream. They have bodies, tails, wing pads, gills to breathe with, and legs to swim and crawl.

When the nymphs reach maturity, they will swim to the surface or crawl to the shoreline. We refer to this stage as the *emerger*. This movement makes the nymphs vulnerable to the fish. Some of the emergers struggle to rid themselves of the nymphal shuck, taking longer to get to the surface, and the fish take every advantage of these situations. The insects that successfully emerge are now adults, and the wing pads split open, allowing the two sailboatlike wings to unfold. They ride the surface, unable to fly until their wings are dry. At this stage too they are very vulnerable.

The mayfly adult has no mouth—it can't bite or sting. Its sole purpose is to mate and reproduce. Fly fishermen refer to this first of the adult stages as the *dun*.

With wings dry, the duns leave the water and fly to the stream bank, where they will rest under leaves of trees or brush. During this rest period, the duns will go through another transformation, shedding the adult skin. They are now called *spinners*.

MAJOR EASTERN HATCH SEQUENCE—MAYFLIES

NAME	COMMON NAME	SIZE	APPROX. DATE
1. *Baetis vagans Cingulatus*	Blue-Winged Oliver	16 & 18	4/10 to early May
2. *Epeorus pleuralis*	Quill Gordon	12 & 14	4/21 to 5/21
3. *Paraleptophlebia adoptiva*	Blue Quill	16 & 18	4/23 to 5/21
4. *Ephemerella subvaria*	Hendrickson	10 & 12	4/25 to 5/25
5. *Ephemerella invaria rotunda*		12 14	5/15 to 6/14
6. *Stenonema vicarium*	March Brown	10 & 12	5/15 to 6/14
7. *Stenonema fuscum*	Gray Fox	10 & 12	5/21 to 6/21
8. *Ephemerella dorothea*	Sulphur	16 & 18	5/30 to 6/20
9. *Epeorua vitera*	Sulphur	12 & 14	6/3 to 7/2
10. *Ephemera guttulata*	Green Drake	6 & 8	6/3 to 7/4
11. *Isonychia bicolor*	Dun Variant	8 & 10	6/10 to 7/7
12. *Ephemerella cornuta*	Blue-Winged Olive	14	6/7 to 6/20
13. *Ephemerella attenuata*	Blue-Winged Olive	16 & 18	6/14 to 7/7
14. *Stenonema ithaca canadense*	Light Cahill	10 & 12 12 & 14	6/14 to 7/21
15. *Ephemera varia*	Cream Variant	8 & 10	6/21 to 8/7
16. *Potomanthus distinctus*	Cream Variant	8 & 10	6/21 to 8/7
17. *Ephemerella lata*	Blue-Winged Olive	16 & 18	7/5 to 8/1
18. *Pseudocloeon carolina dubium*	Tiny Blue-Winged Olive	20 & 22 24 & 26	May, Aug. & Oct. July, Aug. & Sept.
19. *Tericorythodes atratus stygiatus*	White-Winged Black	24 & 26 28	Late June to Mid Sept.

The noticeable difference one sees between the dun and spinner is that in the spinners the tails are longer and the wings have changed from a solid or mottled color and now look almost glassy and transparent. The male spinners usually leave their resting place first, flying out over the water, gathering with other male spinners in cloudlike clusters. They begin a mating dance, with sometimes hundreds of spinners gracefully rising and falling above the water. The females will appear, enter the cloud of males, and choose a partner. They then copulate in the air, and the female returns to the water to deposit fertilized eggs. The eggs drift to the bottom and eventually evolve into the immature mayfly nymphs. The spent female spinner floats on the surface, once more easy food for the trout. The male spinner may mate again, but he, too, will soon fall to the water and die. This entire cycle, from nymph to spinner, may take from a few hours to a few days, depending on species.

When a fly fisherman says that a certain fly is hatching, he means that the flies are hatching and flying from the water: This is the *emergence*. When he talks about a *spinner fall*, he is referring to the spinners coming back to the water to deposit their eggs and die.

The wise use of a hatch chart will prepare us for a particular hatch. Some insects are the same both in the East and West, others may have different common names in different parts of the country, and still others may be present on certain streams in certain regions. A good fly shop or regional book will have hatch charts for reference. For instance, our chart for eastern mayfly hatches (see page 97) shows us that in the spring on most rivers, the hendricksons (a type of mayfly) hatch. So, at this time of year, we should always have Hendricksons in our fly box ready to use should we encounter the hatch.

A trout's behavior can change during a hatch of insects. An opportunist by nature, the trout is almost always looking for something to eat. During a hatch or spinner fall, when there are thousands of identical insects available, trout can become *selective*, focusing on the specific available insect.

CADDISFLIES

Caddisflies are the energetic insects of the stream bottom. They have three stages: the wormlike *larva*, the *pupa*, and the tentwinged *adult*. In some cases, the larva can be a real homemaker—building an underwater home out of minute pieces of stream debris. Like the mayfly, caddis live in their underwater world for about a year. When they emerge, the larva transforms into a pupa. Also like the mayfly, they are vulnerable to the trout in this stage.

But unlike the mayfly, who has to dry its wings before flying, the caddis is usually immediately airborne. Sometimes, though, the pupae have trouble shedding the larval shucks and float half-in, half-out of the water with the shuck trailing behind, still attached. Any struggle on the surface will surely attract the fish. After hatching, the adult caddis migrate upstream, often in great numbers, cloud after cloud moving together above the water. Caddis, like mayflies, are harmless and will rest before mating. On Montana's Bighorn River, I have seen caddis hatches so thick fishermen can't open their mouths without eating caddisflies!

When the adult caddis lay their eggs, they often skitter around on the water, expelling the eggs. Some species will actually swim back underwater to deposit their eggs on the stream bottom. At all times during egg-laying, they are available to the trout.

Caddis hatches occur regularly throughout the year; others seem to pop up sporadically. The adults usually have mottled brown, gray, or tan wings, and one of the biggest hatches in the West is black. The Henryville Caddis mentioned earlier works well for almost all caddis adults except the black. For the black, you need a more exact imitation with a black body and wing. In the air, caddisflies look like tiny moths.

STONEFLIES

To many people, large mature stonefly nymphs look prehistoric. They appear to be armor-plated with two distinct wing pads (mayflies have one), and two tails (most mayflies have three). Often nocturnal in the East, this insect requires fast, well-oxygenated water. Stoneflies have two stages: nymph and adult. When mature and ready to hatch, the nymphs usually swim to the shoreline and climb out on exposed rocks or the bank itself. The nymphal shuck splits open, allowing the adult to emerge. The adult's wings lie flat over the back.

The stonefly, like the mayfly and the caddis, is important in the trout's diet and is harmless. Stoneflies hatch sporadically throughout the spring and summer. In the West, anglers wait patiently for the dependable spring stonefly hatches that bring up some of the biggest fish of the year.

MIDGES

Midges include the tiniest of insects and some that bite, including mosquitoes and gnats. Midges have three stages—larva, pupa, and adult—and play an important role in trout fishing. Active year-round, they are sometimes the only game in trout town. At times, when they are migrating in the surface film by the thousands, it becomes necessary to imitate them. The midge pupae hatch in the film and the adults swarm over and on the surface to lay their eggs. Often imitated on size 20 or smaller hooks, midges are sometimes referred to as "the angler's curse" because the small flies are difficult to tie on the leader and to see on the water. The Griffith Gnat, in a couple of small sizes, is a good fly for imitating adult midges.

TERRESTRIALS

Terrestrials are any of a large number of landborn insects that find their way into a trout stream. Ants, beetles, grasshoppers, crickets, leaf rollers, moths, and caterpillars fall or are blown into the water. When aquatic insect hatches are sparse during the hot summer months, terrestrials help fill the void in the trout food chain. Actually, many of these insects are available from the time the frost leaves the ground in the spring through the first heavy frosts of late fall. Of all terrestrials, the ant is probably the most prolific, and a black-ant pattern can be deadly fished dry or wet.

There are excellent imitations available for all of these insects. Start with the flies that you expect to use first depending on season or region. Ask for and rely on the advice of other fishermen and fly shops. There are excellent books from which to learn more about these and other insects (see suggested reading). There will be times when the fish are more selective and harder to catch than at other times. But with a basic knowledge of insects and a few good flies, you'll be well on your way to hooking them!

WARMWATER FLIES

When these insects are found in warm water, they become food for bass and other fish, as well as for trout in cold water.

For six favorite bass flies, I consulted Bob Clouser, owner of

Clouser's Fly Shop in Middletown, Pennsylvania. Bob lives near the Susquehanna River and spends his summers guiding fly fishermen for bass.

Bob lists the following flies as his all-time favorites (four are his own innovations): Clouser Deep Minnow, Clouser Crippled Minnow, Clouser Crayfish, Clouser Swimming Nymph, Popovics Banger, and Lefty's Deceiver. Bass flies are often large and are sometimes designed to cause a disturbance on the water to attract the bass. The Crippled Minnow and the Popovics Banger are fished on or just in the surface of the water. The others are fished underneath at varying depths.

All warmwater fish are fun to catch on flies. A day this past summer comes to mind, when a friend and I started catching catfish on Clouser Minnows. It was great fun to watch them follow the flies to the surface and then, at the last second, take the fly. Perch, pickerel, sunfish, and catfish all are a lot of fun for the fly fisherman.

ABOUT THE HOOK

Being able to make the correct fly selections requires a little knowledge of the hook. As illustrated, a hook has an *eye*, *shank*, *bend*, *point*, and *barb*. The most common design has a straight shank with a turned-down eye. The eye allows us to attach the fly to the leader. The hook point is designed to penetrate quickly and should be kept sharp. Look at your hook every so often when fishing to

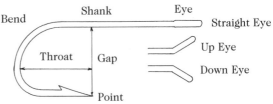

The parts of a hook.

make sure it's not tangled around the leader and that the point is okay. Sometimes, if our backcast hits the weeds or stones behind us, the point will break off, and this may go undetected until a fish is lost.

The purpose of the barb is to help the hook hold once it has penetrated. There are pros and cons on the subject of hook barbs. The barb can do a lot of damage to the fish when we

The smaller hook is barbless.
Compare the barb on the large hook.

remove the hook. This is especially true of freshwater fish, whose mouth tissues are often softer than that of some saltwater species. If we plan to release our fish, pinching down the barb on the hook will cause less damage to the fish, and the hook will be easier to remove. The barb can easily be pinched down with a pair of needle-nose pliers. Some hook manufacturers offer hooks without barbs, but they are expensive, so most flies are tied on hooks with barbs.

Hook manufacturers offer a variety of hook styles to help fly tiers imitate certain insect and baitfish patterns. Hook shanks may be longer or shorter, thinner or thicker, or the shank may be curved to give the fly a certain look. The eye may be turned up or may point straight ahead. If the hook is intended for saltwater flies, it will probably be of stainless steel to resist corrosion.

Fly sizes correspond to hook sizes. Hooks are sized by numbers: as the number increases, the hook size decreases; a size 18 is much smaller than a size 10. Most common freshwater hook sizes go from 1 through 28. Hook sizes larger than 1 use an 0 designation and, as their numbers increase, so does the hook size. So a 4/0 hook is larger than a 1/0. For a fly fisher interested in trout or panfish, a general hook range would be sizes 8 through 16. When you look at hook sizes 16 and smaller, it's hard to imagine that you can actually hook and land a fish on such a small hook. In reality, smaller hooks can penetrate and embed better than the larger, heavier hooks.

Most fly fishermen sooner or later take up fly tying. It's a natural progression and can add a new dimension to the sport; catching a fish on a self-tied fly is rewarding. But beware of the friend who tells you that tying your own flies will save you a lot of money. Fly tying is an addictive hobby. Whereas a fly fisherman can easily spend hours browsing through accessories, reeling reels and flexing rods in a tackle shop, a fly tier finds it just as easy to spend hours looking through furs, feathers, hooks, and vises. There is always a new material or tool to try. Someone discovers that pantyhose makes a great wing material, that a makeup brush's bristles work well for tail material, then the rest of the family shockingly discovers that clumps of hair are missing from the family pet, and so it goes. Fly tying is creative and a good way to pass some of those long winter nights.

It's difficult to describe the pleasure you'll experience when you've chosen the correct imitation and you find yourself suddenly connected to the fish on the other end of the line. Understanding insects and being observant about them will help you become a better, more productive fisherman.

7

FINDING AND PURSUING

FISH WHERE THE FISH ARE! BUT WHERE ARE the fish? Good fishermen develop fish sense. Learning the needs and habits of our quarry will help us know where to find them.

Like all creatures, fish like to feel safe in their environment. The rule of nature is eat or be eaten, so the first thing most fish do to survive is take advantage of any available cover. Cover can be many things—a submerged rock ledge, undercut banks, fallen trees, weed beds, shade from an overhanging tree limb. Fish will take advantage of every opportunity to hide from enemies. They will find cover in unexpected places, such as under boat docks and high-way bridges. I remember a small brown trout that was hiding in an old truck tire at the bottom of a pool in the Delaware River, and a smallmouth bass that found shelter in an old metal drum in the Susquehanna River. Depth can also be a source of cover. Fish will feed near their cover whenever possible.

Understanding the needs of the fish will make us better fishermen. Although freshwater species often share the same likes and dislikes, they are all unique.

TROUT

Rated high on the list of popular gamefish to catch on a fly, trout require cold oxygenated water. A trout's body temperature is determined by the water temperature, and its metabolism and digestive system also work in line with water temperature. When these temperatures drop below fifty degrees, trout can become dormant, loosing the urge to feed actively. The same condition can occur in warmwater temperatures. Water temperatures that exceed seventy degrees will put the trout off. If the water should reach eighty degrees, its survival is in question.

How will this information help us find the trout? Well, we now know trout need cold water. In early spring and fall, when evening and nighttime air temperatures can drop water temperatures below fifty, trout will not move much until late morning or early afternoon, when air temperatures start to warm the water. At this time of year, our best fishing will be during the warmest part of the day.

Late spring and early summer may be the trout's favorite time of year. With water temperatures ranging from fifty to seventy degrees, it is a happy creature and will feed throughout the day.

The warmer water temperatures of the hot summer months can once more change its feeding habits. Now, in the heat of the day it will seek out deeper, cooler water and shaded areas, waiting for cooler evening temperatures. The best fishing will be in the very early morning hours and late afternoon and evening, after the sun is off the water.

Warmer water temperatures mean less oxygen. Because trout need oxygen, during summer weather when water temperatures rise, look for the trout in the riffles and runs, where the swift currents can produce the much-needed oxygen.

A typical tailwater fishery.

TAILWATER AND SPRING CREEKS

Tailwater fisheries and spring creeks are two exceptions to typical trout-stream conditions. Manmade impoundments or dams with bottom cold-water releases have actually created blue ribbon trout rivers. Two examples are the reservoirs on the Upper Delaware system in New York State and the Yellowtail Dam in Fort Smith, Montana. Deeper water is always colder water. With a bottom-release tailwater dam, a controlled amount of cold water is released on a daily basis to maintain constant water flow and temperature. When this is done, we create the optimum environment for trout.

A serious concern always on the minds of the fishermen fishing tailwaters is the unexpected release of water, causing the water levels to rise, sometimes drastically and quickly. There have been many instances when fishermen have been stranded on the wrong side or on islands when the water rose, and they couldn't get back across the river. Keeping an eye on the water level around the rocks by the side of the stream should alert you to any increase in the water flow.

Unfortunately, we occasionally fail to do our part with water releases. Shutting off or cutting back on water releases during the hot summer months can have a devastating effect on the trout population. But for the most part, bottom-release dams provide us with some wonderful fishing opportunities.

Spring creeks are jewels when it comes to trout water. Most trout streams depend on annual rainfall to supplement their water levels. These streams start out as a number of small seeps that merge to form a stream. We call these *freestone* streams. Spring creeks, however, often originate from large underground springs and are often located near large veins of limestone. The combination of cold water and limestone results in mineral-rich cold water and consistent water temperatures, providing ultimate trout habitat. Because of the high alkali content in spring creeks, aquatic vegetation is often abundant. This vegetation provides not only a diversity of food for the trout but also convenient hiding places.

THE TROUT FAMILY

The American Fisheries Society recognizes ten different species of trout in North America. But the rainbow, brown, and brook trout are the most popular with fly fishers.

A nice rainbow (above).　　　　　　　　　　　　*A fertile spring creek.*

The beautiful brook trout.

The rainbow is easy to identify by the pinkish lateral line on the sides of the fish. Rainbow trout range throughout most of the United States and are indigenous to the Pacific Coast. They spawn in the spring and can be found in both lakes and streams. When in moving water, they seem to prefer the faster riffles or runs.

The brook trout, although linked to the trout family, is really not a true trout at all, but a *char*. Native to many coldwater streams, brook trout are distinguished by their orange and white fins. The back of a brook trout is a camouflaged combination of olive-green and black, and with pale yellow and red spots on its sides, the brook trout is a pretty fish.

Often smaller than the rainbow or brown, the brook trout makes up in beauty what it lacks in size. Brook trout spawn in the fall and are commonly found in the upper reaches or headwaters of many trout streams.

The brown trout found its way to America from Europe in 1883. It quickly adapted and is found in most trout water throughout the lower forty-eight states. Like the brook trout, brown trout spawn in the fall. Color patterns may vary depending on the environment, but generally a brown trout has a tan to dark brown back, lighter tan to silver sides with black or red dots. Equipped

The brown trout.

with a pea-size brain, a brown trout can often outsmart the best of fishermen. It is shy and selective and will test the best angling skills.

TROUT TACTICS

Catching a trout on an artificial fly can be challenging. As fishermen, we are the trout's predator. And a good predator is always cautious in approach.

Never wade into the water without first looking ahead for fish. Trout can feel vibrations and are by nature very nervous. They can see shapes approaching and will quickly head for cover. Once alerted, a trout will not be fooled into taking a fly.

A trout will break through the water surface when it takes a floating insect. We call this a *riseform*. Look for the telltale saucer-sized swirl on the surface. When a trout takes an insect sitting on the surface, there should be a few air bubbles in the dissipating swirl. If you notice only the swirl and no bubbles, the fish is probably feeding on insects just under the surface.

There will be times when just the rear fin or the tip of the tail breaks the surface: we call this *tailing*. This type of feeding activity happens frequently on spring creeks where trout are rooting in the aquatic vegetation, looking for insects.

Trout often cruise shorelines looking for smaller fish. Minnows usually move in groups or schools. When a trout moves on a school of minnows, the smaller fish will flee in fright, often skipping across the water surface. Watch for the wake from the trout in the water behind the fleeing minnows.

When you approach the water and see no feeding activity, take a minute and study the water. Locate the areas that provide cover. If the water is clear, try to look for fish holding near the cover. With good polarized sunglasses and clear water, you may soon be able to pick out a fish or two.

SEARCHING THE WATER

Unless you're entering very clear shallow water and can see that there are no fish where you're about to wade, make a few casts, covering the water just to be sure. Sometimes we find fish where we don't expect them to be. Making a couple casts first will only take a minute, and you might be surprised at what turns up.

Casting systematically, cover all the likely looking water: start close and work your way out, using progressively longer casts before moving to another spot. Because surface feeding activity is

often limited to a few hours when aquatic insects are hatching, using searching patterns when there are no rising fish can be very effective. Underwater flies like the Clouser Minnow or the Woolly Bugger are good search patterns.

When conditions are right, trout will take a dry fly even when there are no insects hatching. An Adams or a Royal Wulff are two good choices. Don't be afraid to experiment and change flies often. If you are not having any success on the surface, try a fly underneath, perhaps a Hare's Ear Nymph fished deep along the bottom.

DURING THE HATCH

Hatches of aquatic insects like mayflies or caddisflies can occur within a few hours' time or sporadically throughout the day. Trout will take advantage of these hatching periods and will feed on the adult insects floating on the water surface. Choosing a fly that resembles the hatching insect in size and color is called *matching the hatch*. Be careful, though—the insect a few yards away may look quite different up close. Most aquatic insects trout feed on are harmless—don't be afraid to take one in your hand for a closer look.

Watch how the insect behaves on the water and try to imitate this behavior. If the adult insect is moving or fluttering around on the water, then you may want to try skittering your fly. On the other hand, if the insects are lying still on the surface, you'll want your fly motionless as well. The key to successful fishing during a hatch is being able to imitate the natural insect with an imitation—in appearance and behavior.

The underwater stages of insect activity are the hardest to detect. Preceding the actual hatch

In this cutaway view of a trout stream, the arrow indicates the direction of the current flow. The fish are facing into the current; notice how the flow is carrying food toward them. The deep area in the middle is a pool, and there are riffles on either side of it.

(or emergence) of the adult insect, there will be a period of under-water activity at the nymph or larval stage. These underwater counterparts to the adults will be swimming to the surface, and the trout will feed on them.

Most of the time, because of depth or water clarity, it is impossible to see this underwater feeding activity. But there will be other times when conditions are right and you'll see the silvery flash from a trout's side as it takes an insect under water. Being observant means looking *into* the water as well as *on* the water.

TYPES OF TROUT WATER

Trout can be found in both still and moving water. Although I enjoy trout fishing in lakes and ponds, my first love is the moving currents of a trout stream. To me, moving water has character, charm, and appeal.

Most trout streams and rivers are made up of *riffles* and *pools*. Riffles separate pools and are composed of faster-moving water that is generally shallower than that of the pool. Velocity of flow is obviously related to topography. Depending on the make-up of the stream, some riffles will be composed of fast currents broken up by large rocks or boulders. This type of water is commonly called *pocket water*.

Pools are the deeper areas where the current is generally slower. Fishermen refer to pools as having a *head* and *tail*. The head is where the fast water, usually from a riffle at the top, meets the deeper water of the pool. The tail is at the downstream end, where the water starts to get shallow; the stream may start to get narrow and gain speed, going into the next riffle.

The lengths of riffles and pools vary from stream to stream. A small mountain stream may have riffles ten feet long and pools about the same size. A larger river can have riffles and pools a half mile or longer, again depending on the topography.

Lakes and ponds are sometimes cold enough to support trout. They, like streams, must be fertile, with a food chain of insects and baitfish for a trout's sustenance. Most lakes have shallow shelves that drop off into deeper water. Trout will often cruise these shelves looking for food but will return to the deeper water for cover and safety. Many lakes and ponds are fed by coldwater streams. These can be productive areas to find trout, because the current carries in colder oxygen-filled water as well as insects.

WILD VERSUS STOCKED

Wild trout are natural treasures. Wild trout have hatched from an egg in the natural coldwater environment. They often survive against the odds: global warming, acid rain, industry pollution, natural predators, building development, the list goes on and on. It's easy to understand why blue ribbon trout streams are in decline. Yet they do survive. It's a very special feeling to hold a wild fish, to admire the colors, the fins, and to think of its will to survive. But the reality is that fly fishing and fishing in general are popular, and there are more fishermen than our remaining wild trout streams can support. So we have introduced stocked fish.

Most states have stocking programs. The trout are raised in hatcheries and put ("stocked") in the streams and lakes when they reach a certain size that is determined by the individual states.

The trout is a wonderful creature, deserving of our respect. It can be extremely difficult to catch, and on more than one occasion I have cast repeatedly to a rising trout, watching in frustration as it refused each of my offerings. We have trout in our local catch-and-release stretch so selective that they actually touch the fly with their noses before deciding to accept or refuse. And at times I've watched them follow and even refuse the naturals!

SALMON AND STEELHEAD

Salmon and steelhead are also coldwater species that fly fishermen hold in high regard. There are three different groups of salmon: Atlantic, Pacific, and landlocked. All three are born in fresh water; two migrate to the sea to spend part of their lives and then return to fresh water to spawn. But only one will return to the sea after spawning.

The Atlantic salmon is considered by many to be the king of the salmon, for he is born in fresh water, migrates to the salt, returns to his birthplace to spawn, and once more returns to the security of the ocean.

The Pacific salmon has similar habits except that it will only return once to fresh water, where it will spawn and die. There are six species of Pacific salmon, and five are found in North America: pink, chum, sockeye, chinook, and coho. The sixth is the cherry salmon, found only in northern Asia.

The landlock is an Atlantic salmon that is simply trapped

The Atlantic salmon.

inland. With no access to the ocean, most landlock salmon spend part of the year in freshwater lakes and the balance in the cold-water streams that feed the lakes.

Both Atlantic and Pacific salmon have little interest in feeding when they migrate into fresh water to spawn, yet they will take flies. There are many theories as to why. One theory is that they can be teased into taking, and another is that they are simply angry at anything that gets in their way. I guess it's not important to solve the mystery, because these are magnificient fish to catch on a fly rod.

Steelhead, like salmon, are migratory fish living part of their lives in the ocean or in deep lakes or reservoirs. These are ocean-going, often large, rainbows who return to birthplace rivers to spawn, and like salmon, they will take flies. On summer steelhead rivers of the Northwest, there can be exciting dry-fly fishing when these fish rise to the surface for flies.

Steelhead frequent the wild rivers of the Pacific Northwest, Alaska, and British Columbia. Recent introductions to the Great Lakes have expanded their availability to the angler.

Most salmon and steelhead fishing is done with underwater flies, although there are times when Atlantic salmon or steelhead can be teased to the surface with a dry fly. Searching the water with brightly colored underwater-fly patterns seems to work best. It's important to get the fly to the fish. Because these migratory fish often hold in deeper water, a sinking-tip or a fast-sinking fly line may be needed. Patience is a virtue with this type of fishing.

LARGEMOUTH AND SMALLMOUTH BASS

Warmwater species, these popular gamefish can be found in lakes, rivers, and ponds. Both the largemouth and the smallmouth are efficient predators and feed on a variety of smaller baitfish, worms, crayfish, frogs, and insects. They are members of the sunfish family.

There are three distinct ways to tell a largemouth from a smallmouth bass. First, the dorsal fin (the fin that runs behind the head and continues back toward the tail) on a largemouth is shorter and does not continue to the tail, as does the same fin on a smallmouth. Second, the mouth on a largemouth is much larger than that of a smallmouth. And third, the color of a largemouth is dark green to almost black, whereas the smallmouth is more of a

A smallmouth bass.

tannish bronze. Some anglers call the smallmouth "bronzeback."

The largemouth likes a weedy environment, which provides both food and cover, in which to live. Lily pads make excellent overhead cover. Working the edges of the lily pads with a surface popper will often produce nice largemouth bass. They'll hit hard and cause quite an explosion in the water.

Largemouth bass are solitary fish and prefer still water to moving water. They can survive in a variety of water conditions but prefer warm, shallow lakes and ponds. Largemouth bass are spring spawners and during the spawning period become extremely territorial. Interestingly, it is the male largemouth and not the female who guards the nest until the eggs have hatched.

Smallmouth bass are often compared to trout by fishermen. Both thrive in moving water, their diets are similar, and both take flies well. The smallmouth, often smaller than the average largemouth, makes up in strength what it sometimes lacks in size.

A good smallmouth-bass river or stream varies little from a good trout stream. The basic difference is often the water temperature. In some rivers, the smallmouth bass and trout share the same water.

Smallmouth spawn in the spring of the year. They feed on and below the surface. Casting small foam surface poppers to streamside weed beds to search the edges or looking in fast-moving riffles with an underwater search pattern is a lot of fun. Be sure to put bass on your list of fish to catch.

PANFISH: BLUEGILLS, PERCH, ROCK BASS

Panfish, or crappie, as they are often called, are also members of the sunfish family. Panfish flourish almost everywhere, from backyard ponds to warmwater lakes and reservoirs. They love insects and are fun to catch on a fly rod, providing great sport for the new fisherman. Any fly that will catch a trout will catch panfish, so fly selection is easy.

PIKE AND PICKEREL

Long-nosed and nasty, pike and pickerel often share the same water with bass. Pike will aggressively strike a fly, and with a

A panfish

mouthful of razor sharp teeth they can tear a fly to shreds. Similarly to bass, pike like weed beds for food and cover and will cruise the shallows in search of smaller fish, the main course in their diet. They will take a swimming frog, a small duck, and at times, even attack a muskrat swimming on the surface.

When fishing for pike, I like to cast a streamer and retrieve it quickly on a floating line. A wire tippet section in front of the leader makes good sense, because the sharp teeth of a pike or a pickerel can bite through monofilament. And be extra careful handling these fish—use long-nose pliers to remove the fly.

The pike.

GETTING AROUND

A BIG PART OF THE APPEAL OF FISHING FOR me is that we can fish in all kinds of water. In fresh water, we have ponds, lakes, reservoirs, streams, and rivers. Salt water offers flats, channels, and bays. In order to effectively fish in all of these situations, we will need different modes of water transportation. There are many choices to consider, depending on our specific needs and requirements.

Regardless of what vehicle we choose to help us get around on the water, safety should always be foremost in our minds. By taking a boating safety class, the angler will not only learn how to safely operate a boat but will better understand currents and flows, what to do in emergencies, and how to prevent a bad situation from becoming a disaster. If you're near salt water, you'll learn about incoming and outgoing tides, wind, and weather; you may learn to read a navigational map, and maybe some first-aid. A class of this type will help you become more adept around any type of watercraft—and you never know, the life you save may be your own. Safety should never be taken lightly.

Going out a few times with someone who is experienced with the type of watercraft you're using can be a big help. Letting an experienced person show you the ropes will save you a lot of mistakes—some of which can be very costly. Safety aside, the shortcuts alone you can learn from someone else will save a lot of time. I know—I tried to teach myself to paddle a canoe and didn't know for months that I was facing the wrong direction and had the wrong paddles. It took an experienced canoeist to tell me these things—and I thought I was coming along pretty well!

Up until just a few years ago, our choices in watercraft were pretty limited. We could consider a boat, a canoe, a raft, and more recently a float tube. We now have all kinds of inflatables available. Depending on the kind of water you're going to be on most often, the type of vehicle you drive (in order to transport it), and your budget, there is a type of watercraft available today that will fit anyone's needs.

For awhile, we'll be happy walking the edges of our favorite stream, flat, or pond to get to the fish. But before long we'll start thinking that the really big fish are too far out in the deep water for us to reach, or that if we could just get to other side the fishing would be better. If we're on a saltwater flat, we have to keep the tide in mind. If the tide is coming in, we may not be able to get back, or there may be narrow, deep channels that we can't cross, and, again, the fish are always on the other side! Well, now we *can* get there.

INFLATABLES

One-person inflatables have a lot of advantages for fishermen. They are easy to transport and, deflated, take up little room in the car. They quickly inflate with a foot pump and are lightweight and easy to carry to the water. They can be powered with a set of fins, and in some cases have oars. Inflatables are available in lots of different models and prices.

FLOAT TUBES AND U-BOATS

Every time I think of the construction of a float tube or U-boat, I am reminded of the infant walkers that were so popular years ago. The person who invented the first float tube must have been a mother. The seats on both a baby's walker and the float tube are identical. If you picture an inner tube instead of a tray, you've got a float tube.

Float tubes have come a long way since first being introduced many years ago. Today they are safer, better-constructed, and have more features. The tube is actually two or three separate bladders that are individually inflated. There is usually at least one bladder for the backrest, and that is also inflated separately. The rubber bladders are covered with a heavy-gauge denier nylon that resists tears and punctures. In the event that one bladder should be punctured, the other inflated bladders will be enough to get you to shore.

Depending on the model, it may have zippered external pockets for fly boxes, lunch, and other accessories; there may be Velcro rod holders to fasten the rod to the tube for changing flies or working on the leader; an O-ring for a net; and even an anchor! (Don't laugh, it's hard to stay positioned with just the fins on your feet.)

Stocking-foot neoprene waders are best when using a float tube, because the waders are stretchy, warm, and comfortable. Instead of wading shoes, I like to put a pair of neoprene socks on and then my fins. The socks protect the feet on the waders from sharp stones when you are walking in and out of the water. Most fins today will float to the surface if they work loose from your feet. Otherwise, the fins should be tied with cord or shoe laces around the ankles so they don't go to the bottom if they come off!

Because the float tube is donut-shaped, it can be tricky getting your feet through the leg openings when wearing the fins. But getting the fins on with the tube around your middle is even more difficult. The only person I've ever seen fall out of a tube was trying to get in it! Go slow and take your time. Once you're in, and near the water, it's easy to walk backward to the water. It's very hard to go forward because of the fins, and when you look down, you can't see your feet because the tube is in the way. Slowly back in, to just above your knees, and sit down in the seat. You'll be afloat, and if you paddle with your fins, you can move along easi-

Fishing from a float tube.

ly. Remember, you'll be going backward, so you have to keep an eye behind you to stay on course.

The U-boat came along a few years after the float tube. As the name indicates, a U-boat is shaped like a horseshoe, with an open end. The seat is similar to a float tube's, but it's much easier to get in and out of. Once the fins are on, you can back out into a couple feet of water, and with the U-boat behind you, take hold of the two ends and pull them forward around you. Sit down, and you're in! Most models have quick-release seatbelts to hold you in place, and a mesh apron that attaches in front, providing a work area. The fly line can also lie in coils on the apron when it's not being used.

The U-boat, and similar designs, offer the same features as the float tube. U-boats tend to be a little heavier and more awkward to carry, but they are easier to fish from in the water. Having the open front end makes landing the fish easier. Reaching over the tube is sometimes difficult.

Fishing from the float tube or U-boat is a unique experience. What I remember most from the beginning, is being down low in the water. The ducks and turtles didn't scurry away in fright. And the birds alongside the stream continued chirping and singing. It was as though I was being accepted into their homes and becoming part of their environment. I enjoy tubing even when I'm not fishing.

PONTOON BOATS

Water Otters, Float-and-Totes, and Kick-Boats are all popular. Much larger than a float tube or a U-boat, these watercraft offer rowing platforms that are attached to two inflated pontoons. The area between the pontoons is open to the water so you sit on a seat with your legs down in the water, or you can rest them on the frame. Pontoon boats are easy to get into and can be picked up easily and carried over shallow riffles.

Most pontoon boats feature a lightweight aluminum rowing platform or have oarlocks on the pontoons. The oars are a great asset on windy days or in water with current. Along with the oars, the user wears fins to fine-tune positioning. If you want to stop in shallow water, you simply stand up between the pontoons, and the boat stays with you because the frame is around you. I can make quiet easy turns with my fins whenever I need to change my casting position. An ice cooler attached to the rowing platform behind the seat makes a great place to store extra gear.

Getting into a U-boat.

SAFETY FIRST

Regardless of design, these one-person inflatables should always be limited to still or slow-moving water. They are not designed for fast water, and although most models have at least two inflatable bladders, you may want to have with you some form of personal flotation device. Some state laws require that you do, so make sure you know the regulations where you are fishing. Inflatables are all vulnerable to wind, so use common sense on windy days. It may be real easy going out across the lake—but you have to come back, too. If there are waves on the water, look for a protected cove and don't go out on the wide open water. If it's real bad, wait for a better day!

If you're fishing large reservoirs or areas where boat motors are allowed, wear bright clothing and be alert for these boats. You're going to be hard to see, and they may be going fast. Stay fairly close to shore, and leave the deep water for the motorboats. Look for areas that only allow electric motors; they are quiet and slow—and safer. Don't stay out after dark. Not only will you be impossible to see, but the shore can look all the same and you may not be able to find the take-out spot. Put a waterproof flashlight in one of your pockets and look for landmarks on the shore that you'll be able to recognize at dusk.

CANOES AND BOATS

The canoe is one of my favorite ways to be on the water. Although I'm not an expert at handling a canoe, and I'm still hesitant to take along anything that shouldn't get dunked, I still love to be in one. To me, a canoe is almost romantic. It's quiet and easy to maneuver on calm water and can go in very shallow water.

We have a fairly wide canoe, which is a little more stable than most. And we've learned some lessons the hard way. For instance, it's easier when there are two people—one to paddle the canoe and the other to fish. And keep all the loose items in a bag and tie the bag to a seat. As a matter of fact, tie everything down, including the cooler. Know where the boat cushions are and always have a change of clothes in the car! It's amazing how fast a canoe can tip!

Our canoe is fiberglass. I can lift it and carry it a short distance, but I can't get it on and off the roof rack of our van by myself. Aluminum canoes are a little lighter and easier for one person to handle. Weight is a major consideration for the person fishing alone.

A view of the back of a pontoon boat.

As romantic and quiet as a canoe is, most of the time I am in a boat. There is always lots of room so you can move around easily and be comfortable. Some boats have padded seats, or you may sit on boat cushions. There might be storage compartments for extra gear, and maybe even a casting platform for the fisherman. You can be fairly certain that the camera and binoculars will stay safe and dry. The bow may be carpeted, and there may be rod holders on the sides.

A small rowboat on a bass pond may be equipped with a set of oars. On the other hand, the boat you take to the local lake may have oars and an electric motor. Electric motors are good for a few hours, and then they need to be recharged. An extra battery can be taken along for additional time. These motors are quiet and easy to operate, but they don't have a lot of power. They should never be used in situations where thrust and power are needed.

A boat on a big river or lake may require an outboard motor. Outboards run on gas, and an extra tank of gas can easily be taken along. A lot of things can go wrong with outboard motors, and someone in the boat should have experience in running boats and operating motors.

Casting from a canoe.

Depending on the size of the boat, a boat trailer may be necessary to transport it. Some small boats can be put on a roof rack, or in the back of a pickup truck for short trips. Unless there is a boat trailer and a winch, two people are usually needed to get the boat in and out of the water.

My father has gone to Canada to fish every year for many years. When my sister and I were little, Dad and Mom would pack tents, cooking utensils, food, ropes for tree swings, swimming things, and all of Dad's fishing gear (including his boat), and off to Canada we'd go.

Looking back, what I remember most about Dad fishing is that on the last day he would take Mom, my sister, and me for a ceremonial boat ride, and he would try to fish. All week, up to this point, we were happy to stay in camp, play on the swings, swim in the river, and do all the exciting things kids do. Mom would read, sit in the sun, settle disputes, and watch us play.

But this last day was always something else. Of course, we were restless and we couldn't sit still in the boat. Every time we'd move, we'd kick Dad's tackle box, knock something off the seat, or drop something in the boat. Dad would firmly tell us, in his not-so-patient fatherly voice, to sit down and be still, that we were scaring the fish. Mom would sit in the back of the boat and read a book, trying not to get involved. Needless to say, nobody enjoyed that boat ride, my father included, I'm sure. In retrospect, we should all have sat down and talked about it. We would have enjoyed our last day in camp, and Dad would have enjoyed his last day on the river.

All boats, but especially aluminum boats, transmit sound. Fishermen have to be careful not to move coolers, kick soda cans, or drop fly boxes in the boat. Even a rod sliding off the seat and the reel hitting the bottom of the boat can scare the fish. Wear rubber-soled shoes and keep loose items stored so they aren't making noise.

Before you take off in a boat, know where the boat cushions are in case of an emergency. Put a strong flashlight in your gear bag and make sure someone in camp knows you're going out and when you'll be back. If you're late and they're watching for you, signal with your flashlight and have them signal back to give you an exact location on the camp.

Take a good look around and locate a couple of landmarks that you can see from a distance. If you're on a big lake, it's easy to get turned around and lose your bearings. Pretty soon you don't have any idea which way camp is. Locate where the sun is in rela-

An aluminum bass boat.

tion to the camp. Just knowing the camp is on the west side of the lake and remembering that you passed an island on the way out will help you find your way back.

A float tube, pontoon boat, canoe, or boat are all great ways to enjoy fishing and the outdoors. Keep an eye on the weather; watch for storms and wind. Head back to camp if it looks like bad weather is coming your way. If you're inexperienced, stay close to shore for a while, and go a little farther out each time. As with everything, stay alert to what is going on around you and use common sense. Any type of watercraft can provide many hours of fun and pleasant memories.

HOOKING, CATCHING, AND RELEASING

HOOKING YOUR FIRST FISH IS AN EXCITING experience. Imagine that! A fish has actually taken your fly! It's happening, and you've waited so long! No amount of mental preparation can prepare you for the moment. If you are fishing a dry fly, you'll see the fish take the fly. A moving strike indicator, used when fishing a wet fly, is also a visible "take." With a retrieved fly you will feel the pull or strike when a fish takes the fly.

Immediately after the fish takes the fly, we respond by *setting the hook*. For freshwater fish, a quick lift of the rod tip should hook the fish. How hard or fast we lift is difficult to say, partly because the answer depends on the size of

A trout coming up to take a dry fly on the surface.

the leader material and also the size of the fish on the other end.

When a fish takes the fly, it realizes instantly that the fly is not an insect after all and will do exactly what you or I would do—try to get rid of the hook.

Rod-tip position is important in setting the hook. The rod tip should be low to the water, almost never pointing upward. Do not point the rod tip directly at the fly. Instead, keep the tip at a slight angle and just a couple inches ahead of the fly whenever possible. When a fish takes and we set the hook, the angle of the rod tip will help cushion the strike. If the rod tip is pointed at the fish, you'll have a direct connection between the fly and the fish. If you strike too hard, the leader will break and you'll loose the fish.

I remember one of my first trout on a fly rod. It was a wild brook trout about six inches long. It engulfed an Adams dry fly. In my excitement, I struck so hard the little trout came flying back over my shoulder and ended up suspended in a tree. I felt as bewildered as the fish looked dangling helplessly from the low limb. Well, setting the hook is part of learning, and like most things, experience is the best teacher.

Some saltwater fish require more than a tug on the rod to set the hook. Fish like tarpon, with jaws that seem impenetrable, often require all the strength we can muster to make the hook hold. Under these conditions, I like to strike off to the right side with the rod in my right hand, at the same time quickly pulling the fly line back in my left hand. This helps drive the hook point into the muscular tissue in the tarpon's mouth (see chapter 11).

If you are fishing with a saltwater guide, you may be instructed to "hit him again." This means repeat the striking motion several times to insure that the hook is securely embedded. At this point, you'll either be thankful that you ran the hook over the hook hone or you'll be wishing that you had. Sharp hooks penetrate deeper and quicker. It's more important on big stainless-steel saltwater hooks than on smaller freshwater hooks, but some of the best fishing advice anyone can get is to keep hooks sharp.

Saltwater fish will almost always hold on to the fly longer before expelling it than will a freshwater fish. So the reaction time to the strike can be slower. In fact, it's often better if you hesitate for a moment before striking. Since most saltwater fishing is with flies that are retrieved, the fish will be coming straight at the fisherman. If the water is clear, it's easy to get trigger-happy and strike before the fish has a good hold on the fly. It takes a lot of discipline to hold back until the time is right.

Okay, the fish is on—what next? Keep cool; there are a number of things that can happen, depending on the size of the fish and on how much room he has to run.

FIGHTING A FISH

First of all, it's necessary to keep some tension on the line. You should always feel the fish on the rod. If there is a lot of slack line, the fish will be able to shake his head to throw out the hook. But if there is too much tension, the leader will break. There may be a few coils of slack line in front of you; if so, this needs to be recovered as quickly as possible. Slack line will almost always cause trouble. Keep the rod tip elevated and off to the side, exerting pressure on the fish. If you're right handed, the line should be in your left hand.

If the fish is strong enough to pull this slack line out through the guides, let him do so. A smaller fish may not be strong enough to "run line," and this extra line should be reeled back on the reel. Learn to play the fish from the reel. I doubt there's a fisherman anywhere that hasn't learned this lesson the hard way. If most of the fish you catch are small fish that can't run line, it's easy to strip the line in by hand until you can reach the fish. While the hook is being removed, all the slack line just lies out in front, and with a small fish this line is not a problem.

But then along comes a big fish and we strip the line in as always, and when it decides to take off we have slack line lying all over, getting tangled up around the reel, around the gadgets on our

vest, around ourselves, and there's never been such a mess! Of course the leader breaks, and the fish is lost.

Once the slack is either used up by the fish running line or by you getting it back on the reel, the fish can be played from the reel. The fish can still run line off the reel, and as it tires or turns toward us, we can reel the slack line back onto the reel.

If the fish is running line, the drag on your fly reel will apply tension on the outgoing line to slow the fish. If your fly reel has an external rim, additional pressure can be applied to the line by palming the reel (see chapter 2).

Never grab the reel handle while the fish is running line. If it's a strong fish, the handle will be turning so fast that your knuckles can be bruised. Maybe worse than skinned knuckles, you'll break off the fish.

I remember Barry several years ago shouting at a beginning fly fisher who had a big fish on to "let go of the handle." Well, the woman, who had a death grip on the reel handle, suddenly responded and let the entire rod drop into the water. Barry took off downstream in hot pursuit of her tackle. He got the rod back, but the fish was gone. He asked her why she let go, and she diplomatically reminded him that he had shouted at her to let go of the handle. Of course he meant the reel handle, not the rod—but he didn't say *which* handle.

If the fish jumps, it's important to lower the rod tip to put a little slack into the jump, which we hope keeps the leader from breaking. As soon as the fish is back in the water the rod tip should be lifted to pick up the slack, and we can then continue to play the fish from the reel. Saltwater fly fishermen call this technique *bowing* to the fish. By lowering the rod tip and reaching toward the jumping fish, you add a controlled amount of slack.

When you're able to land the fish, be sure to keep some line out beyond the end of the rod. If you reel in too much line then, the fish will be at the end of the rod and you won't be able to reach that far. Keep in mind how long the rod is and allow for the length of the rod plus a couple more feet of line beyond the tip. For instance, if your rod is eight feet long, ten feet of line and leader out of the rod will be just about right. This will give you enough line to land the fish without providing any extra in which to get tangled.

When the fish is ready to land, by bringing the rod back toward your shoulder and having the net ready in the other hand you can guide the fish into the net. Since the net will be in one

The right way to play a fish: The rod is bent, all slack is gone from the line, and hands are in the proper positions on rod and reel.

*Just about to successfully land a trout: Slack is gone from the line,
and there's just enough line out to bring the fish to the net.*

hand and the rod in the other, the line should be under a finger
against the rod handle. Otherwise, the weight of the fish may pull
unwanted line off the reel. These last few seconds can be critical.
Sometimes the net startles the fish and it will make one last bolt
for freedom, and you need to be ready for this. If this happens,
remember to let the line slide out through the rod hand. At this
point, you can tuck the net under your arm so you have both
hands free to play the fish and bring it back again to the net.

To net or not to net? Whenever I'm fishing in fresh water
along a shoreline, wading in a stream, or fishing from a boat, I use
a net. I have better control of the fish when it is in a net. Fish are
slippery and hard to hold, but once it is in the net, I can work with
the fish and quickly remove the hook. I like to keep the fish and
the net in the water and, if the hook is barbless, it comes out easily with a pair of pliers or forceps.

Only a couple of times come to mind when I don't use a net.
In Alaska, the trout and salmon are too big for our nets. When
they are close, we simply reach out with a pair of needle-nose pliers and remove the hook. We seldom have to touch the fish, and
they seldom need any help recovering. When fishing from a skiff

The fisherman is carefully removing the fly from this grayling's mouth with forceps.

in salt water, the guide will usually reach out for the fish when it comes to the boat and remove the hook. With bigger fish, we can usually use heavier leader which brings the fish in quicker and it will not be as tired as when it is played for a long time.

Be careful in handling fish. Trout are very delicate; they need to get back into cold water as soon as possible. Often fish will have teeth, so don't put your fingers in the mouth; use forceps or needle-nose pliers. Beware of sharp fins on panfish and bass. The dorsal fin, on the top of the fish, can be smoothed down by sliding your hand from the nose back in order to get a good grip.

RELEASING FISH

Fish seldom swallow the hook when a fly is used. Therefore, since the hook is usually around the outside of the fish's mouth, it is easy to remove. This fact makes catch-and-release fishing very popular among fly fishermen.

An exhausted fish may need a few minutes to recover before swimming away. You can help by holding it gently and facing upstream in the current until it's ready to swim away. Watch for a

This fisherman is gently cradling a brown trout in the water, making sure it is ready to be released.

minute after you've let go to make sure it stays upright. If the gills aren't working, gently move the fish back and forth in the water with one hand cradling it under the throat and the other holding it around the tail.

All fish should be handled carefully and kept in the water as much as possible. It's easy to injure a fish internally by squeezing it too tight. Gills can be damaged by our fingers, and fish can injure themselves by flopping around at the water's edge. Trout can sometimes be made more manageable if you turn them belly-up.

If you're fishing with someone and you want a photograph of your fish, ask your companion to focus the photograph while you hold the recovering fish under the water. When your companion is ready to push the shutter release button, then lift the fish out of the water. Thus, the picture is taken and the fish has only been out of the water for a few seconds.

Many of the best places to fish remain the best because of catch-and-release policies. It is easy to kill off the biggest and the best of a species, and soon we hear stories of "the good old days when fishing was so much better than it is now." Unfortunately, this is true too often. I don't care to carry dead fish, and I don't like to clean fish. On the other hand, there are some fish that I do like to eat. So I will occasionally help catch bluegills for a fish fry or a snook for dinner. But for the most part, I release my fish. Besides, it makes me feel good—I know there will be more fish left for another angler, or another time.

10

FRESHWATER FISHING TECHNIQUES

IN ALMOST ANY FISHING SITUATION, PRESEN-
tation is the key to success. We can have the right fly, be
in the right place at the right time, and even have feeding
fish in front of us, but if our presentation is poor, the fish
will probably refuse our fly. To be consistently successful,
we need to understand how to fish the various types of
flies we carry in our fly boxes and also how to handle different fishing conditions.

TOP OR BOTTOM?

We have two choices when it comes to flies: we can fish on
top of the water with dry flies or fish underneath the water

with wet flies. Most anglers like dry-fly fishing because it's visible. You see the fly, you see the fish take the fly, and the flies are delicate and easy to cast.

But the truth of the matter is that fish do most of their feeding underneath the water. They will feed on the surface when the food is on the surface, but these times are limited. Yet the fascination with seeing the fish take our fly while it's floating on the water remains.

Some fly fishermen are partial to dry-fly fishing and refuse to fish any other way. These fishermen are nicknamed "dry-fly purists." If dry-fly fishing makes someone happy, there is nothing wrong with fishing this way exclusively, except that it severely limits productive fishing time. To be a well-rounded fly fisherman, we should be comfortable in any fishing situation, be it on the top or on the bottom.

An overhead view of the quartering upstream cast. The arrow indicates the direction of current flow.

My first trout came on a dry fly. Actually, I missed a lot of fish before I finally hooked one. It was a warm late-April afternoon on my home stream, Fishing Creek, and a mayfly hatch was in full swing. Adult insects (duns) were floating on the water, and the trout were feeding on these insects.

My casts were landing too far above the fish or too far below, some were too close, others not close enough. Finally, a cast landed just right, slightly ahead of and in line with one of the rising trout. My fly floated down and the fish inhaled it. I was so excited I forgot to strike. Another cast or two and the fish quit rising. I moved on, looking for another rising fish. This time I overreacted and struck too soon, clearly missing the fish. Finally I settled down and got my act together. I was ready when the next fish took my fly, and a minute later I was holding my first catch—a ten-inch brook trout. I couldn't have been happier, and I was hooked on dry-fly fishing. It's still my favorite way to fish.

One of the most important things to remember in dry-fly fishing is to always keep your eye on the fly. It's so easy to get distracted. You can make ten casts or more, and nothing happens. Another ten go by with the same results. A bird flies over and you look up to watch, a squirrel or chipmunk gets your attention, or maybe you just drift off in thought. And then you look back and your fly has disappeared. You see the telltale riseform and realize that a fish took your fly! You strike, but it's too late. I think the fish know when we look away for just a second, and that's when they decide to play the game. As hard as it sometimes is, we need to concentrate on the fishing at all times.

Most of the time when we're fishing dry flies, we cast quartering upstream (to about eleven o'clock) and let the fly float downstream until we pick it up to cast again. Fishermen who are fishing dry flies will often work their way upstream, whereas fishermen who are fishing wet flies usually work their way downstream. Of course, when I see a fish, I will move into position and cast to that fish. But when I'm simply covering the water hunting for the fish, I like to start with short casts of fifteen to twenty-five feet and use a little more line with each additional cast. This way, I'm working my way slowly across the stream and won't be scaring fish by casting my fly line over them.

DRAG

Unwanted tension on the fly line and leader can defeat us every time. Water in a stream or river moves, and we call this movement *current*. Currents vary in speed and character. Large submerged rocks, depressions in the stream bottom, and underwater weed beds are just a few of the things that can affect the direction and path of the current.

A natural insect floating on the surface will drift with the speed and direction of the current. The insect is just floating along, and we call this a *natural free drift*. But the imitation, our fly, is attached to a leader and the leader to our fly line. If we draw the fly line and leader tight, tension is put on the fly, which causes it to act unnaturally. Our fly will no longer be in a free drift. The unwanted tension can make our fly speed up and drag across the surface, resulting in a drift that looks suspicious to the fish.

An easy way to check for drag is to watch your fly in relationship to other floating objects—insects, floating pieces of leaves, even bubbles that are floating along with the current. All these objects, including your fly, should be floating at about the same speed. If your fly is passing everything, there is drag resulting from too much tension.

What can we do about drag? Casting a very straight line and leader and keeping it too straight on the water will quickly cause drag. A few simple curves or waves in our leader will reduce tension on the fly and allow it to float longer before dragging. Eventually the fly will drag anyway because all the line slack will be used up in the drift. But we want to delay this inevitable drag as long as possible. If we can accomplish this, we will be covering more water with fewer casts—we will be more effective.

The length of our tippet can be one of the keys to a drag-free float. Remember that the average tippet is eighteen to twenty-four inches long. If the tippet is too short, it may land straight on the water, resulting in instant drag. On the other hand, if the tippet is too long, the cast may not have the strength and energy needed to turn over, and the fly will collapse on the leader (see chapter 4).

The position of the rod tip after the cast is made is crucial to a drag-free float. Lifting the rod tip during the drift will immediately pull on the fly line and leader, taking out the needed slack and resulting in drag. The dragging fly passes over the feeding fish and is refused. As soon as the cast is on the water, keep the rod tip low and move it downstream with the fly until it's time to pick up to make a new cast.

Wiggling the rod tip as you complete the forward cast will also add slack to the cast. This movement will put curves in the fly line as it falls on the water. Another method is to tug back on the rod tip as the forward cast is turning over. Although I find it hard to be accurate with this technique, it will add curves, or slack, to the cast.

Perhaps the most popular method is an up- or downstream mend. *Mending* line means throwing a curve in the fly line just beyond the rod tip. The goal here is to reposition a section of fly line without disturbing the fly. After you have put a curve in the fly line, return the rod tip to its original position and follow the drift of the fly (see chapter 5).

SKITTERING AND DANCING

There will be times during egg-laying or hatching when the insects are "skittering" or moving on the surface. During these times, our flies should imitate the behavior of the insects.

Make sure your fly is dressed with fly floatant so it stays dry. Next, watch the insects and try to imitate their behavior with your fly. Keeping the rod tip low and twitching it will skitter and dance the fly. The twitches should be short and intermittent, depending on the desired effect. Stiffly hackled spider patterns, bushy Wulffs, and Elkhair Caddis are good surface search patterns and are easily skittered and danced on the water.

Bass, pickerel, and most other freshwater gamefish can be coaxed to take a dry fly. Because they are not necessarily looking for insects, these aggressive fish will often take a popping bug or a mouse pattern retrieved across the water. If a mouse, injured frog, cricket, or large beetle gets into the water, it will kick and struggle for a few seconds, then rest, then struggle again, in an effort to get back to the edge of the water. When imitating this behavior with a fly, think about the actual struggle of the live creature.

NYMPH FISHING

Aquatic insects spend much of their life under water, living among the rocks, weed beds, and silt. At this stage, these insects are always available to the fish. Nymphs and larvae quickly become a food source when they are dislodged from the stream bottom and drift with the current. Like the adult insect that we imitate with a dry fly, the nymphs and larvae drift free with the current. And like our dry-fly imitations, we need to present our underwater imitations so they look and behave like the actual insects. By mending our line to add slack, we can help our fly drift free with the current speed. Nymph fishermen call this underwater drift a *dead drift*.

In fast-moving riffles, where the current is quickly using up the slack, several mends during the drift may be necessary. The fisherman needs to imagine how the fly is behaving under the water. If it is moving too fast as a result of a tight line and not enough slack, additional mends will add needed slack to slow down the drift, allowing the fly to look more natural.

If you're fishing deep fast-moving water, the additional mends will also keep the fly deeper. The tension from a tight-line cast will not only make the fly speed up but it will also cause it to be pulled toward the surface.

Most dead-drift nymph fishing is done along the bottom where the insects live and where the trout can easily get to them. When we are using a floating line, which is my preference, we

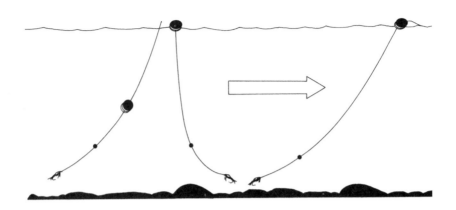

The relationship between the strike indicator and split shot. The arrow indicates the direction of current flow. Left: This strike indicator is too close to the split shot, and it has been pulled under. The fly is dragging, as well. Right: This strike indicator is too far from the split shot, and it has moved ahead of the fly, causing drag. Center: Here is the proper relationship of indicator to shot: There is no tension from any of the parts.

must add weight to the fly or the leader to make it sink. Fly tiers can add weight to the fly by wrapping lead wire around the shank of the hook before the fly is tied. Most fly shops offer both weighted and unweighted fly patterns. Another method, and my favorite, is to add weight to the leader.

Rivers and streams vary in depth, and as I fish through a pool, I am often readjusting the amount of weight on the leader to keep my fly near the bottom. If you find that you're constantly getting stuck on the bottom, you probably have too much split shot on the leader. On the other hand, if you don't have enough, you'll be going over the top of the fish and won't be down where they can see your fly.

There are also times, in the process of hatching, for instance, when underwater insects will be drifting close to or just under the surface. If I am fishing a fly that is weighted, that weight cannot be adjusted, but I can adjust the weight on the leader so the fly will be where I want it in the water.

The most difficult part of dead-drift nymph fishing is detecting the strike. Because we have intentionally added slack to the cast, we may not be able to feel the fish take the fly. A strike indicator attached to our leader will signal when the strike occurs. When a fish takes a fly drifting under the floating strike indicator, the indicator will hesitate, move slightly upstream, or bob under for an instant. It's very much like watching a bobber when fishing with bait.

There will be many times, in using a strike indicator, when we will strike in vain. Whenever the fly brushes against a stone, stick, or tree root, the indicator will be telling us to strike. Sometimes the current itself will play games and make the indicator react. But if we don't strike every time the indicator moves, we may not be striking when it is a fish!

As important as it is to adjust the split shot, it's equally important to change the position of the strike indicator, for the indicator can affect how deep the fly is drifting. If the indicator is too close to the split shot, it may be pulled under from the weight, or it may itself pull the fly to the surface. If the indicator is too far away from the fly, it won't be able to detect the fish taking the fly, and we won't get a signal. If the indicator is too far from the fly, this will also make it easy for the current to move the indicator ahead of the fly, causing drag. In almost all cases, the indicator should be in line with the fly.

Overall, the drift depends on the weight of the fly and split shot in relation to the strike indicator, taking into consideration the speed of the current and the depth of the water. Generally, if the water is four feet deep, your strike indicator should be about six feet from the fly. Allow for the stream depth plus a couple of feet. As you work your way along the stream, moving from riffle to pool and back to riffle, you will be adjusting both the position of the split shot and the strike indicator.

When it is near time to hatch, the nymphs are active in the water. Sometimes they are moving along the bottom. At other times they are struggling in their ascent to the surface. And occasionally they will fall back in their struggle to emerge.

With this in mind, it is logical to assume that the fish will take our nymph as long as it is imitating the natural. In lakes and ponds, fish will often take the fly on the initial descent, as it is sinking. They will also take it as it is being slowly retrieved back to the surface in imitation of the struggle to emerge. But they very seldom take when the fly is hanging suspended from the strike indicator. The natural nymph is just never found in this position, and it simply looks suspicious to the fish.

After the cast is made, be alert for the strike as the nymph is falling. Once it has reached the level where it is just hanging, start a slow retrieve to imitate the struggle. Because fish will cruise in a pond, you'll want to work different areas and experiment with

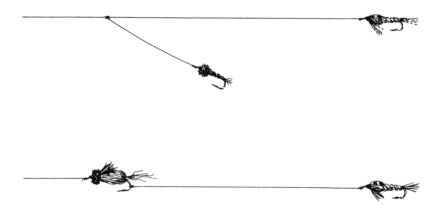

Top: *A dropper, leading from the tippet's connecting knot.* Bottom: *A trailer, attached to the fly hook's bend.*

fly patterns and depth until you locate the fish.

To imitate a hatching or swimming insect, we need to retrieve our fly. When nymphs and pupae are emerging, the insect is swimming up from the bottom of the stream. We need to get our fly down, close to the bottom, and then retrieve it back to the top, thus imitating the natural. In moving water, I like to cast quartering upstream and quickly put a mend in the fly line. The slack will give the fly time to sink and will allow the dead drift to continue until the cast is slightly downstream, or in a quartering down-stream position. At this point (keeping the rod tip low and slightly ahead of the drift), start to retrieve the fly. After a few retrieves, pick up the line and cast again.

Each retrieve should be three to four inches long, and of varying speed. Experiment by starting with a slow retrieve, mix in a few medium-fast retrieves and an occasional fast retrieve. As the nymph swings around below, lead it slightly with the low rod tip. During this swing, the fish will sometimes strike the fly. In some cases the fish will actually hook themselves, but you still need to respond by lifting the rod and setting the hook.

There are times when the fish are feeding on emerging insects just under the surface. Watch for swirls or riseforms without the air bubbles that appear when a fish takes a floating insect. When this type of feeding is taking place, position yourself upstream of the fish and cast the fly about five feet ahead of the fish, allowing some slack in your fly line so the fly can start to sink. When you think your fly has drifted to where the fish can see it, start your retrieve and tease the fly in front of the fish. You

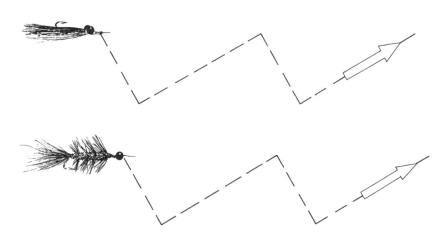

The up-and-down jigging motion of streamers with lead eyes. The fly on top has lead eyes; the one on the bottom has a split shot pushed right up against the hook eye.

probably won't see your fly, but if you see the swirl from the fish taking something, strike! It may be your fly, and you may see the swirl before the indicator moves.

As you fish in different parts of the country, you'll learn different tricks from fishermen you meet on the water. And sooner or later, you'll hear about *droppers* and *trailers*.

Dropper fishing has been around for many years. It is a technique used to fish two flies at the same time. A dropper is usually a short piece of monofilament (six to ten inches) leading off the surgeon's knot where the tippet is attached. When the knot is tied, one tail is not trimmed off, and to this tail is attached a fly.

At the other end of the tippet the second fly is tied. Often the tippet will be a little shorter than usual to help prevent the two flies from getting tangled in casting.

Trailers are a more recent version of the same idea. With a trailer, the fly is tied on the end of the tippet, as usual. But onto the hook bend is attached a piece of monofilament (six to ten inches) with a clinch knot. A second fly is attached to the other end. Trailers are easier to cast, and surprisingly, fish can be caught on either fly. You would think the fish would be hard to hook on the fly in the middle, but in fact one fly seems to be as effective in hooking fish as the other.

Sometimes the first fly will be a dry fly, followed by a nymph. The dry fly can act as the strike indicator for the nymph, as well as a second fly to catch the fish.

FISHING STREAMERS

Fishing streamers is a game of casting and retrieving and covering water. Streamers are great search flies, and they often catch big fish. Most streamers imitate smaller baitfish, but they can also imitate sculpins, leeches, crayfish, and other creatures living in the water that fish eat. Once a fish grows to adult size, it will take more than a diet of insects to keep it happy.

Always keep water temperatures in mind, because they will often be the key to how fast you retrieve and how deep you fish your fly. Cold water temperatures may put the fish on the bottom, and your fly will therefore have to be down deep. Those same cold temperatures may make the fish reluctant to chase anything that's swimming fast, so the retrieve speeds may need to be slow and deliberate.

Most of my favorite streamer patterns have weighted eyes. The lead eyes (of nontoxic material) make the retrieved fly swim in an up-and-down jigging motion. I have caught just about every fresh- and saltwater species of fish using this technique. If the streamer doesn't have lead eyes, or if I think it needs even more weight, I use split shot on the tippet. With the lead eyes, I put the shot about six inches from the fly. If the fly doesn't have lead eyes, I put the shot up against the fly, as close as possible to it, so I can still get the jiglike motion when I retrieve. In deep water I may use additional split shot farther back on the leader, but there is always one against the fly. Streamers work in almost any water condition, but they are especially effective in water starting to discolor after a rain shower.

Streamers can be fished in almost any direction, but my favorite is a quartering upstream cast with a quick retrieve, then a straight-across-stream cast and a retrieve followed by a quartering downstream cast and a retrieve. If the streamer appears to be staying near the surface, I'll add a couple of mends before starting the retrieves. Sometimes I'll wait five to ten seconds before retrieving to give the fly a chance to sink deeper. Repeat these casts three or four times, and then take a few steps downstream and start over again. This is good search strategy, and it can cover a lot of water. Often the fish will take or chase the streamer during the first two or three casts. After that, they usually lose interest.

Because we are constantly moving the fly with our retrieves, we don't need strike indicators when fishing streamers. When the fish hits a moving streamer, we feel the bump or "smack" on the line and instantly respond by striking and setting the hook.

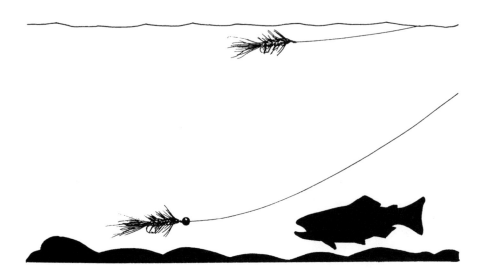

Proper depth can be achieved by weighting streamers with split shot.

Change patterns often; if one fly is not producing, try something else. My favorite streamer color is black, but after ten or fifteen minutes of fishing any pattern without results, I will quickly switch to something else, or adjust the split shot. Don't be afraid to experiment until you find a winning combination.

11

SALTWATER FLY FISHING

THE OCEAN HAS ALWAYS FASCINATED ME
—the marine life, the spaciousness, the sounds. It is an
inviting place. In the fly-fishing world, it's the new fron-
tier, for there are new places to explore and species of fish
yet to be caught. There's a lot of ocean out there waiting
to be explored.

Here in the Northeast, we have striped bass, bluefish,
bonito, mackerel, and many others. Weakfish, or sea
trout, are popular adversaries, as are redfish along the
mid-Atlantic. San Francisco Bay offers great striped bass
fishing, too. The Florida coast gives us bonefish, tarpon,
and permit for starters. In the backcountry you'll find snook,

redfish, and baby tarpon. Snapper, jack crevalle, false albacore, barracuda, cobia, ladyfish, rockfish, and sharks join the list. In deep water we have marlin, tuna, sailfish—why, the opportunities are endless!

Fly fishing in salt water is very different from fishing in fresh water. The fish are stronger—*much* stronger. A brown trout caught in fresh water may weigh eight pounds, and it will put up a good fight. But an eight-pound bonefish in salt water will out-fight, outrun, and outdo the brown trout in every way!

It took years of coaxing to get Barry to try saltwater fly fishing. A friend, Jack Gartside, kept twisting his arm, and finally he gave in and we went. Well, when we realized that flats fishing is a lot like trout fishing, we were hooked. We were still sight-fishing, stalking, and casting to shy fish.

I quickly realized that saltwater fly fishing was going to be quite an adventure. In the years since then, salt water has opened up for me a whole new arena in which to play the game of fly fishing. And I love the weather. It's not hard to leave single-digit temperatures in December or January to find balmy eighty-degree days filled with sunshine, blue skies, warm water, and fish.

TIDES

Tides bring water in and take water out, and water levels fluctuate with tide changes. Most saltwater gamefish feed on other fish, mostly smaller baitfish. These baitfish migrate with the tides. Larger fish will take advantage of situations when the tide makes baitfish available. By understanding tides, we can often put ourselves in the best fishing locations, and at the right time of day, when larger fish will be looking actively for smaller fish.

The moon and the sun affect the tidal flows. Both exert gravitational pull on the earth. But the moon's pull is nearly two and one half times greater than that of the sun. Water is pulled toward the moon as it travels on its orbit around the earth. It takes the moon twenty-eight days to travel along this elliptical path. There are times throughout this period when the moon's distance to the earth changes. The farther away the moon is from the earth, the less pull it has on the water, resulting in lower tides.

There is a twice-monthly period of seven days when the moon is closest to the earth. At this time, the sun and the moon are in a nearly direct line with the earth. The positions of the three bodies increase the gravitational pull, which causes tides to rise higher and fall lower than at any other time within the month.

We call the tide at this time a spring tide. As the moon continues its orbit, it is positioned at a right angle to the sun, and for the next seven days the difference between high and low water is at a minimum. We call this tide a *neap tide*. In the next seven days there will be another period of spring tides, which will be followed by another week of neap tides. Then the cycle is repeated.

Incoming tides normally provide the best fishing. Tide charts and predictions are available from local tackle shops and newspapers. Tides not only bring baitfish to larger fish, they also can have an affect on water clarity. Wind or storms may discolor the water, but a tidal change can take away the dirty water and replace it with clear water. Tides can also have an effect on water temperature. It's obviously important to understand tidal fluctuations.

FLATS

Flats are areas of relatively shallow, even depth, mostly ten feet or less, with either a hard or a soft bottom. If you snorkel over a flat, the bottom might look like a miniature lunar landscape. There are craters, valleys, and depressions—places for small creatures to hide. In some areas there will be underwater grass, called turtle

A typical shallow saltwater flat.

grass, which provides a hiding place for both predators and prey. Flats range in size from that of a football field to larger areas that encompass miles. Flats are often interlaced with deeper channels. All flats have edges, places where the shallow water levels drop off into much deeper water.

Flats are often connected to shorelines, but they can also be completely surrounded by deep water. They have their own ecosystems, and some are healthier than others. The more activity a flat has, the better the fishing. Besides the baitfish, flats are nursery grounds to a variety of creatures. Crabs and shrimp are two primary flat dwellers and are favorite foods of the bonefish and permit. On a healthy flat, birds will patrol overhead and wade the shallows, looking for an easy meal. If you see evidence of smaller fish, the odds are that the larger fish are not far away.

There are two ways to fish a flat. If the bottom is soft and mushy, you'll need a boat. If it's hard, you can wade. Like most inshore saltwater fishing, wading a flat is a game of searching—wading slowly, always watching, looking for movement, like a predator.

Whenever you're wading, a pair of neoprene flats boots will be a big help. These boots come up over the ankles, giving you protection from sharp coral and helping to keep out sand and grit. They have good soles to protect the bottoms of your feet, and a zipper makes them easy to get on and off.

Be careful when wading—sharp coral can hurt, and stingrays and sea urchins should be avoided. On sandy bottoms, drag your feet forward as you walk. Stingrays have a habit of settling in and disguising themselves in the sand. If your foot touches the edge of a ray, it will be frightened away. If you step down on it, the sharp stinger in its tail may go into your foot. It isn't being nasty; it's just its way of letting you know it's there. Sea urchins have ball-shaped bodies with sharp spines that stick out at all angles, and these spines can hurt, too. While we need to be aware of stingrays and urchins, don't be frightened by them. They are seldom encountered and usually easily avoided.

Sooner or later, you're going to encounter a shark while you are wading a flat. I remember my first experience, when a large lemon shark started to swim in my direction. I was knee-deep in water, and shore was about a quarter-mile away. When the shark was within twenty feet of me, I slapped my rod on the water. The noise immediately frightened it, and it headed for deep water. I've never heard of a shark attacking a fisherman, and I suspect that any predator fish must feel uneasy leaving the safety of deep water to come onto a flat in search of food.

The sun can be an asset or a liability on a flat. When you're wading and looking for fish, always try to have the sun coming forward over your shoulder. If you wade directly into the sun, the glare and reflection make it very difficult to see the fish, even with polarized sunglasses and a good hat.

BONEFISH

Found throughout Central America, the Caribbean, and the Florida Keys, bonefish offer the light-tackle angler a real challenge. Sometimes called the "silver bullet" because of its streamlined profile and unbelievable speed, a bonefish will run all the fly line and put you int the backing before you can blink an eye. They're always on the move and extremely shy, feeding on flats, often in shallow water. Trophy size is ten pounds or more, but even smaller bones are unbelievably strong.

Bonefish travel in schools, pairs, alone, or in triples. The schools are usually smaller fish, while the singles, doubles, and triples will often be big fish. Bonefish are predominantly bottom feeders, eating crabs, shrimp, and small minnows. They are very sensitive to water temperature and feed best when the water is at least seventy degrees. When bonefish feed in low water, they can often be seen tailing. As they root down in the bottom, their tail will break the surface, giving them away to the angler. Traveling bonefish often create wakes or ripples on the surface that will indicate the direction they're traveling.

Rebecca Carey with a bonefish in the Bahamas.

Because bonefish are always on the move, the angler must stay alert and ready to cast in an instant. To cast to a moving fish, the fly should be at least six to eight feet in front of the fish. On a tailing bone, the fly needs to be within two feet. Retrieves usually need to be slow at first, in three- or four-inch strips. If a bonefish follows but hesitates to take, quickly speed up the retrieve.

My favorite bonefish flies are Clouser BP's (bonefish-permit), Crazy Charlies, and our own Beck's Silly Legs, all in sizes 4 and 6. My favorite colors are white, chartreuse-and-white, tan-and-white, and pink. These flies have lead eyes to make them sink, and I like to use eyes in different sizes—when the water is shallow, heavy eyes can land too hard and scare the fish. However, in deeper water the added weight is needed for depth.

PERMIT

This is the elusive fish of the flats. Strange and yet beautiful, permit are the most difficult of the flats fish to catch on a fly. With feeding habits like the bonefish, they, too, cruise in search of crabs and shrimp. Weighing from two to thirty-five pounds or more, the permit has a reputation for charging the fly only to

The author and her guide, Mike Zettles, with a barracuda in Mexico.

refuse it at the very last second. I have watched permit actually touch a fly, tailing like a bonefish, but never actually taking it. The frustration is overwhelming!

My best permit fishing has been in November at Boca Paila Lodge in Mexico. My favorite permit flies are the Clouser BP's and Beck's Silly Legs, both in size 4. The McCrab, a crab imitation, in sizes 2 or 4, is an excellent choice, but I find the other patterns just as effective and easier to cast. Good colors are chartreuse-and-white and tan-and-white.

BARRACUDA

The long, slim profile of a barracuda reminds me of a freshwater northern pike. And like the northern pike, the barracuda has a mouthful of vicious teeth. He hunts the flats, often lying motion-less, waiting for an unsuspecting fish.

With all his vim and vigor, a barracuda is great sport on a fly rod. Once hooked, he'll greyhound across a flat, testing the best of drag systems. Barracudas look and act mean and strike at their prey with a vengeance. With a long profile and distinctive mark-ings, a barracuda is easy to identify in the water.

Unless you're rigged for barracuda, it's probably best not to cast to one. A wire tippet is needed, for a barracuda will easily cut through sixty- or eighty-pound monofilament. It will completely destroy the fly and can be a tyrant in the boat. Reaching over the edge and removing the hook with a pair of pliers, allowing it to stay in the water, is a better idea than trying to handle it in the boat.

Barracuda like large saltwater streamers retrieved very fast—the faster the better. They take great pride in proving that nothing can outrun them. My favorite flies are Lefty's Deceivers in sizes 1/0 and 2/0, in white, red-and-white, and yellow. A Cockroach in sizes 1/0 and 2/0 and a Clouser Deep Minnow in the same sizes in either all white or yellow are also good choices.

TARPON AND SNOOK

Tarpon are the armor-plated bandits of the salt. With big beautiful eyes and bucket-size mouths, they will often follow a fly to the boat before taking it. Once hooked—and they are hard to hook—they often become airborne, jumping to eye level and then running line for fifty or eighty yards before jumping again.

A sixty-pound tarpon is considered small by big-tarpon enthusiasts, and twenty- to thirty-pound fish are called "baby" tarpon. Babies? Well, thirty pounds of tarpon on an 8-weight rod is a real adventure. I have to admit that eighty-pound and larger tarpon are just plain hard work to me, but I never get tired of catching baby tarpon.

When fishing for tarpon on the flats, I like to use saltwater streamers. But if I'm working the edge of a mangrove, a floating popper will bring the tarpon to the surface. Often a wake can be seen coming behind the popper during the retrieve, and suddenly the water explodes and the fish is jumping. It's very exciting.

Snook, on the other hand, tend to be slower and curiously cautious. They will follow the fly right up to the boat and then turn away, while a tarpon will often follow and hit it at the last second. Snook are easy to identify by the black lateral line running along their sides. They range in size from a pound or two up to twenty-five pounds for a big snook. They are good eating and popular in some lodges for an occasional dinner.

Snook like mangroves. They will slowly work along the edges of the cover and watch for smaller fish. Sometimes they can be seen back in the mangroves, and the fisherman must patiently watch and wait for the fish to move into an area where he can hope to get a cast.

Tarpon and snook, like most flats fish, are affected by water temperature and will disappear when the water is cold, only to reappear when it warms up again. When conditions are right, it's action-packed fishing.

My favorite flies for both are Lefty's Deceivers in white, yellow, and red-and-white, and a Cockroach. I like both patterns in sizes

The author with a tarpon in Mexico.

1/0 and 2/0. On the surface, white or red-and-yellow poppers in size 1/0 are good choices for the tarpon.

Setting the hook in salt water. The rod hand strikes to the right and the line hand strikes simultaneously down and back.

SALTWATER TACTICS

Forget finesse when it comes to setting the hook in most saltwater fish. It's a hard quick pull, or draw, on the rod with the slack out of the line. Often, if I am fishing with a guide, he'll yell, "Hit him again," and he wants me to pull again on the rod. Each time you pull hard and fast, the hook point penetrates a little farther and you have a better hold on the fish. It's kind of like "yanking" the leash on a St. Bernard who is determined to chase the neighbor's cat.

Saltwater fishing authors have compared a tarpon's mouth to concrete, so you can see why a sharp hook is needed to penetrate well. To set the hook, I use my left hand to pull the line down and back hard, extending my arm low behind me and sweeping the rod tip low and to the right whenever possible. If the fish jumps, I quickly drop the rod tip, adding slack, and bow to it. If the fish comes down on a taut line, it usually breaks off.

Never let a big fish rest—always keep pressure on it. Worry it, make it move, and keep it working. That's the only way it's going to tire. To turn the fish right or left, drop the rod low to the water and pull, leading it in the direction you want it to turn.

At the last second, when you think it's all over, be prepared for the unexpected. Gamefish have the ability to pull out reserve power and will often make one last bolt for freedom when they see the angler, the gaff, or the net. Make sure any slack line is on the reel, don't have it in your hands, and don't stand on it in the boat. If the fish takes off like a bullet, the line can get wrapped around angles and hands. Play the fish to the end from the reel.

SALTWATER RODS

Fishing in salt water is different from fishing during a hatch on a trout stream. Instead of casting continually to rising fish, a saltwater fisherman does a lot more looking, and then casting. We seldom cast blind, and we spend a lot of time staring at the water looking for moving shadows, nervous water, and tails—and other indications of fish. At the end of a good day bonefishing, my eyes are far more tired than my casting arm.

My favorite saltwater fish are bonefish, permit, and small tarpon. For these fish, my favorite rod is a nine-foot rod for a 9-weight line. Eight-weight rods are often thought of as the all-purpose saltwater rod, but I find the nine a real advantage in turning over larger flies, especially in the wind. And there are very few days in salt water without wind. A 9-weight rod also has better lifting power. When the fish is at the boat, you need to put pressure on the rod to lift it up to the net. A 9-weight will have more "backbone" than the 8. Of course, if you go for tuna, bluefish, or big tarpon, a heavier rod will be needed, perhaps an 11- or 12-weight.

My favorite saltwater flies. Top right: *A Cockroach, surrounded by three Lefty's Deceivers.* Bottom: *Two foam poppers.*

SALTWATER REELS AND LINES

I like an anti-reverse reel that will hold at least a hundred and fifty yards of backing. Remember, with an anti-reverse, the fly line can run off the reel without the handle spinning. I've had too many bloody knuckles trying to get a fish under control with a direct-drive reel. My favorite reels are manufactured by Billy Pate (Tibor Reel Manufacturing) and Lamson. Both are made for harsh salt-water conditions.

My reel will have a floating weight-forward fly line, either Scientific Angler's Bonefish taper or Cortland's Saltwater Lazer line, both intended for salt water. In my gear bag is an extra reel with a sinking line or sinking tip for deep water.

LEADERS

Leaders will vary depending on the fish and the size of the fly. For bonefish, I use a ten- to twelve-foot knotless leader tipped out at 8-, 10-, or 12-pound test. For permit, I use the same length leader and increase the tippet to 15-pound test. For barracuda and blue-fish (fish with cutting teeth), I like a nine-foot leader with a six-inch wire tippet attached. For small tarpon and snook, I use a nine-foot leader tipped out at 18-pound test, and to that I add a twelve-inch shock tippet of 40-pound monofilament. The shock tippet will give additional protection against abrasion. Of course, if the fish are larger, the leader must be heavier.

In most saltwater conditions, we are casting heavy, wind-resistant flies. The leader must have enough muscle to turn over these flies. Saltwater leaders generally have butt sections that are much heavier than standard freshwater leaders. I know very few people who build their own saltwater leaders—it's simply much easier to buy them. Leaders are available with shock tippets attached. With knowledge of a couple of knots, anyone can be proficient in working their leaders.

WIND

Wind has always been my number-one enemy in saltwater fishing. It has defeated me more than once. Wind can provoke casting problems; it can discolor water or create a chop on the surface, making it difficult to spot fish. Stronger wind can blow waves high enough to ground small boats, and more than once I've sat in my room because of small-craft warnings (so take a good book). But wind is a fact of life in fishing, and especially in salt water.

When casting in the wind, try to find a position or angle that will allow you to cast downwind. If the guide can, he will usually position the boat in this direction. If that is not possible, try to make your casts as low to the water as possible. The higher in the air the line travels, the more problems the wind can create.

BOATS

Most inshore fishing is done with a flats boat, or skiff. These boats range in length from fourteen to eighteen feet and are powered by an outboard motor. The front of the boat is called the *bow* and the rear is the *stern*. Flats boats can cross shallow water and have a range of up to one hundred and fifty miles, with an average speed of forty miles per hour. These boats make it easy to move quickly from one place to another. Once you're where you want to be, the guide will use a long pole to silently glide the boat through the flats in search of fish.

A good flats boat may have a casting platform on the bow. The fisherman will stand on the platform, watching, and casting when he sees fish. There may also be a higher poling platform for the guide. Being elevated helps the guide spot the fish, but it may also make it easier for the fish to spot him. The bow will some-times have clock positions painted around the edge. Twelve o'clock is always straight ahead of the boat, nine to twelve will be on the left, and twelve to three on the right. This reference helps the guide quickly point out fish. If he says, "One o'clock, fifty feet," you'll know where to look for the fish.

There are certain precautions to take inside the boat. The floor can be slippery, especially when wet, so move about cau-tiously. Wearing flats boots or sneakers with rubber soles will help. The boots can get hot in the boat, so I always keep a pair of pull-on sneakers handy—the fly line will get tangled up in regular lace-up sneakers. Sound travels faster under water than above it, so care should be taken not to drop soda cans and other items.

When you get up on the bow to cast, strip line off the reel and coil it at your feet, being careful to remove any items that the line can get tangled around. If you find that you're constantly standing on the line, try going barefoot. I prefer it when I cast because I can feel when I'm on the line. But be careful, it's easy to burn your feet doing this!

The author fishing from a casting platform in salt water. Guide Simon Bain holds the skiff steady.

I like to hold the tippet and fly in my rod hand, ready to drop and cast if I see a fish. Once the fish is seen, casting has to be immediate or the chance will be missed.

At the end of the day when your guide is pulling up to the dock, stay seated until you're sure the boat is secure. Step out with a gear bag or empty soda can, set them down, and turn around for the rods. It's tricky trying to climb out of a boat holding the rods. It's easier and safer to have someone in the boat pass them to someone on the dock.

Be prepared for cold boat rides and all kinds of weather. I've seen many perfectly warm sunny days turn absolutely sour miles from the lodge. Regardless of what the day looks like when we start out, I keep a nylon jacket and pants in the gear bag, with a long-sleeved shirt and a hand towel as well. I recall one afternoon in Mexico when everyone in the boat ended up wearing large garbage bags with holes cut out for our heads. We were a sight! But thank goodness we had the bags! Boat rides to and from the flats can be cold, and a jacket will feel good. A waterproof dry bag can hold all the extras you need and can usually be stuffed up under in the front, out of the way.

Pack your bag the evening before, after dinner. Things can get hectic in the morning, and it's easy to forget something. I don't like rushing to get everything together at the last minute. Things that I will want in my bag, as well as the items mentioned, are sunscreen, sunblock for my face and lips, a couple of cotton handkerchiefs (tissues become a mess), Band-Aids, and an extra flats hat with a flap in the back to protect against sunburn, and of course some snacks.

In a canvas tote bag that I can keep on the seat beside me will be my tackle: extra leaders, leader material, fly boxes, knot-tying tool, pliers, hook hone, wire, and so on.

And before pulling away from the dock, look in the cooler and make sure you see plenty of drinks and lunch!

12

WOMAN TO WOMAN: YOU CAN FISH ANYWHERE

FOR THIS CHAPTER, I'VE INTERVIEWED women fishermen all across the country. And what an eye-opener it has been for me. All of the women I talked to fish alone often. The stories and experiences I will recount here are all theirs. I'm not going to identify them for obvious reasons, but they know who they are, and I owe them a debt of gratitude. They are an inspiration to women everywhere who fish and enjoy the outdoors.

I asked each woman the following six questions:

1. Have you had any experiences that relate specifically to women, things that would never happen to a man?

2. Have you ever felt afraid for your personal safety while fishing alone because of another person?

3. Do you have any advice for a woman who is just starting to fly fish and will be fishing alone?

4. Have you ever met any really impolite fishermen as far as stream etiquette is concerned?

5. Have you ever been really afraid when fishing for any reason?

6. Do you think there is such a thing as "woman's intuition"?

Starting with the first question, I have two stories to tell, and they both come from the same woman. I'll call her Jane.

Jane and her husband were with a guide on one of the Great Lakes. They were about a couple of miles out from shore, so there was no land around, but several other boats were close by, within plain view. Jane told the guide that she had to go to the bathroom and asked if he would take her to shore. The guide said the fishing was good, that he would lose his spot if he went in, and that she should use the five-gallon bucket in the back of the boat. She couldn't budge the guide, and her husband shrugged his shoulders with an "I don't know what to tell you" look. So when she couldn't put it off any longer, she used the bucket.

Needless to say, she won't go fishing there again. I am very glad to report that this was the only humiliating incident related to me from over twenty women. And what is humiliating to one of us may not be to another. But I think this would be a very uncomfortable situation for most women. I think the guide should have explained the "bathroom" situation beforehand, and maybe Jane could have done something differently, like going one more time before they left shore, or drinking less coffee and juice at breakfast! No one likes surprises.

Jane's other story takes place along a trout stream when she, once again, got out of the water to go to the bathroom. Well, she got back in the brush along the edge of the stream, got her waders pulled down, and proceeded. But pretty soon something started biting her. She jumped up, pulled up her waders, and trapped red ants inside them. She had positioned herself on their anthill, and when they got wet they came out and started up her waders. By the time they got to her skin, it was too late. After jumping around, yelling, and hitting her waders, she had to take them off completely to get all the ants out. So pick your spot carefully!

Only one of the women could recall a time when she was afraid for her safety because of another person. Katherine was fishing alone in the summer on the Madison River in Montana.

This was a pretty popular stretch of the river close to the highway, but no one else was fishing at the time. There was a steep bank leading down to the water. Once she was in the water she could hear the cars on the highway, but she couldn't actually see them.

Well, she heard car doors slam and assumed another fisherman must be coming down to fish. The next time she looked up, three men with ski masks were hurrying down over the bank about a hundred yards from her. She knew something was up because it was summer (so they weren't skiing), and they didn't have fishing equipment. She ran up the bank with her fly line trailing behind, jumped in her car, and left. She has no idea if they intended any harm to her, but she didn't intend to stick around to find out. Good thinking.

Overall, most of the women thought their cars had a better chance of being broken into than they had of being physically threatened by another person while fishing. If a man is looking for a woman alone, there are just better places to look—the mall, or the parking garage in town. It's sad in one way (that the problem has to exist at all) and reassuring in another (that it isn't a worry during fishing).

All the women said their first advice to a woman starting to fly fish is not to go alone for a while. Too many things can go wrong when you're just getting started, and this is true for men, too. It helps to have someone around to help with the things that will eventually be easier, like crossing the stream or knowing where to fish once you get to the stream.

They also suggested, and I agree, that you start in the no-kill and catch-and-release stretches that are established on most streams. These areas are frequently fished, so the chances are that you'll have other fishermen around. These areas usually have established parking areas, so they are easy to find, and the fishing is usually close to the parking.

One of the women emphasized that we should always tell someone where we're going and when we'll be back. This is good, sound advice for a lot of reasons. If we have car trouble or get lost, if we fall and break a leg or get sick, someone will know where to start looking. This same woman said she has a friend she always tells, and then she checks in when she gets back so her friend knows she's home. Tell a friend or a neighbor that if you're more than two hours late, to start looking. And be considerate—don't take advantage of the situation by staying later than you should.

The author gets ready to net Erny Nowakowski's trout.

Almost everyone thought that, for the most part, impolite fishermen are that way because they don't know any better. Nobody likes to have someone intrude on their fishing. Fishermen everywhere are complaining about crowded streams with ignorant fishermen that slosh through in front of them or wade out in front of others to get their fly out of a bush or cross the stream where someone else is fishing. It's very important to respect another fisherman's territory.

There will be times when the person next to you is catching fish and you're not—and, it is hoped, times when it's the other way around. Most fishermen don't mind being asked politely, "Excuse me, what fly are you using?" More often than not, you'll get a helpful answer and maybe even one of the flies.

Millie Elgaway and bonefish.

Of course, if you slosh over, making a lot of noise, creating waves, and scaring all of the fish, your request won't be kindly received. Slowly approach from behind and on the side he's not casting from; get within a respectable distance, fifty feet or so, and politely inquire. One of the women I interviewed remarked that "most men who fly fish are like gardeners; they are happy to share information and to offer help." I like that comparison and agree with her.

When you get to the stream and find another fisherman, watch for a minute or two. Remember that fishermen usually work slowly upstream or downstream. Don't start ahead of him in the water he hasn't yet fished. After all, he was there first. Step in well behind him in water he has already fished, or go somewhere else. If he isn't moving in either direction, walk up close enough to talk to him and ask, "May I fish below you?" (or above, as the case may be). Then give him plenty of room so you both can enjoy your fishing.

Most of the women said they were annoyed when men occasionally made wisecracks from the sidelines; some said they move away to another spot as a result. One woman, Doris, said she once thought she was being proposed to from a bridge. She was fishing below it and a couple of guys walked out and stood on the bridge, looking over at her. They asked her if she was married. She ignored them. They said she was awfully pretty. She ignored that. They asked if she was fishing alone. She ignored that. Then they said she was a good fly caster. She said, "Thank you."

Having someone approach to offer advice and suggestions when you want them is one thing. But when you want to be alone, this intrusion can be annoying. However, the other party likely has good intentions. Some men can't help but feel that they should help "the little lady," whether she wants it or not. And, granted, sometimes we need help; but there are times when it's appreciated and times when it's not.

One of the women remembered fishing in New York by herself when the water was high and she wasn't used to wading in fast water. A couple of men were fishing nearby, and they were worried about her getting into trouble. They gave her some tips on wading and offered to fish nearby in case she needed help getting back out of the water. Being genuine and showing concern is being thoughtful. We should never assume that because someone shows concern they have another motive in mind.

Another experience came from a woman fishing the Jackson River in South Carolina. She was fishing with her dad and had the right fly. No one else was catching fish, and these two guys kept watching her and moving closer, trying to see what she was using. Her dad was just above her, but he wasn't catching fish either. He was keeping an eye on the two fishermen approaching her. Finally it got the best of them, and they went up to him and asked if he knew what that lady was using. They couldn't bring themselves to ask her! For the most part, fly fishing has been (and still is) a man's sport. We will all have a little adjusting to do as more women take up the sport.

Women fish for the same reasons men fish. Sometimes it's just to get away from people and to experience the quiet solitude that fly fishing offers. It's important for fishermen to listen to first responses. We can all tell when someone doesn't want to be bothered, and we should respect those wishes, men and women alike.

Natta recounted an experience she had on the Flat Brook in New Jersey. It was a Saturday afternoon, fish were rising, and people were coming and going. A fisherman cut right in front of her, acting as if she weren't there, and crossed the stream. She asked him what he thought he was doing. He barked back a disgusting

Casting in salt water.

remark about "women fishermen," and they got into a verbal dispute. Natta, who has a short fuse anyway, told him she wouldn't stand for it. She said this man turned out to be very obnoxious and arrogant and proceeded to ask her who she thought she was. Behind him were two men, not with him, but observing the encounter. Pretty soon they started saying, "Give it to him," and, "She's right, you know." She couldn't believe they had taken her side, and pretty soon the man turned around, got out of the water, and left.

Now, if the man didn't know any better, he should have been embarrassed and apologetic. But this didn't appear to be the case. Before we fly off the handle, we need to ask ourselves if there is any way the other person might not know what he or she is doing. If so, we should handle the situation accordingly. In the above situation, if there was any doubt, Natta could have said, "You're going to put down the fish, would you mind crossing below me?" They could have remained civil, and he would have learned something.

One of the women made the remark that it might feel as if men resent women fishermen, but as it turns out they resent fishermen

who don't know what they're doing. Once we become streamwise, we do resent other people invading our space. We have to remember that sometimes it's not intentional. And we can all learn from these experiences.

All of the women said that what bothers them more than poor stream etiquette is the garbage left behind by other fishermen. Discarded Styrofoam cups, beer cans, monofilament, human waste, and toilet paper are offensive to everyone. If you can't carry it out, bury it. To me, this seems like common sense.

Mother Nature will give you many more frightening moments than other fishermen will. There are so many things that can happen that will put your heart in your throat. And most of them happen because we're not paying attention to what's going on around us.

Thunderstorms sneak up, or you find yourself in water that's too deep and too fast to let you go forward or backward. The fishing might be so good that you stay out in the water until dark, and then you can't find your way back to the car. You discover your batteries are dead in your flashlight. You try not to panic, you start hearing noises in the woods, and it just gets worse.

Because fly fishing is so easy to lose yourself in, it is easy to concentrate so hard on the fishing that you forget to be aware of things going on around you. When we do snap out of it at the last second, the situation may have already reached the serious stage and we easily panic.

This is how a fisherman can be quietly walking behind us along the edge of the stream, minding his own business, and when he gets to us and says, "How's the fishing?" we just about jump out of our boots! We never saw or heard him coming until he spoke. It happens to men and women; but as women, we are forced to be a little more concerned for our personal safety.

Everyone agreed with the concept of woman's intuition. Intuition is a voice inside that quietly talks to us. We don't always listen when we should, but it's often talking long before we move into action.

Maybe men and women have intuition, but I think a woman's is stronger and louder. It makes us aware earlier of situations; and if we listen, we can often head off trouble. It could warn us of a developing storm or against wading too deep to get a cast to the fish. Or it could just be a feeling that we shouldn't or don't want to go down in the gorge today. And we may find out tomorrow that a convicted felon was found there on the same afternoon we decided to stay above it and fish, though we normally go down. Mothers definitely develop this sense with their children, but I believe we all have it to use. After all, being a woman definitely has its advantages.

SUGGESTED READING

Kreh, Lefty. *Fly Fishing in Salt Water.* New York: Lyons & Burford, 1986.

———. *Longer Fly Casting.* New York: Lyons & Burford, 1991.

Kreh, Lefty, & Mark Sosin. *Practical Fishing Knots.* New York: Lyons & Burford, 1983.

Meck, Charles. *Pennsylvania Trout Streams and Their Hatches.* Woodstock, VT: Countryman Press, 1989.

Merwin, John. *The New American Trout Fishing.* New York: Macmillan, 1994.

Samson, Jack. *Saltwater Fly Fishing.* Mechanicsburg, PA: Stackpole Books, 1991.

Whitlock, Dave. *Dave Whitlock's Guide to Aquatic Trout Foods.* New York: Lyons & Burford, 1982.

INDEX